Housman's Poems

HOUSMAN'S POEMS

JOHN BAYLEY

CLARENDON PRESS · OXFORD
1992

Oxford University Press, Walton Street, Oxford OX2 6DP
Oxford New York Toronto
Delhi Bombay Calcutta Madras Karachi
Petaling Jaya Singapore Hong Kong Tokyo
Nairobi Dar es Salaam Cape Town
Melbourne Auckland
and associated companies in
Berlin Ibadan

Oxford is a trade mark of Oxford University Press

Published in the United States
by Oxford University Press, New York

© John Bayley 1992

British Library Cataloguing in Publication Data
Data available

Library of Congress Cataloging in Publication Data
Bayley, John, 1925–
Housman's poems/John Bayley.
Includes bibliographical references and index.
1. Housman, A. E. (Alfred Edward), 1859–1936—Criticism and
interpretation. I. Title.
PR4809.H15B39 1992
821'.912—dc20
ISBN 0–19–811763–9

Typeset by Cambrian Typesetters, Frimley, Surrey
Printed and bound
in Great Britain by Bookcraft Ltd
Midsomer Norton, Bath

Contents

Abbreviations

The following abbreviations are used when referring to Housman's poems:

AP   *Additional Poems*
ASL   *A Shropshire Lad*
LP   *Last Poems*
MP   *More Poems*

The texts used are those given in Christopher Ricks (ed.), *A. E. Housman: Collected Poems and Selected Prose* (Harmondsworth, 1988).

CHAPTER 1

Deaths and Endings

In a review of the *Cambridge History of English Literature*, vol. xi, published in the *Cambridge Review* in 1915, Housman remarked that the author of the chapter on Wordsworth 'does not feel Wordsworth's poetry'. For example, the author (the distinguished French scholar of English, Emile Legouis), wrote that although *The Ruined Cottage* could be called a perfect poem it was none-the-less too distressing and desolate: Wordsworth's usual optimism was not to be found in it. 'For that relief much thanks', observed the reviewer grimly, and added that if *The Ruined Cottage* were indeed 'a perfect poem, it would be exalting and not distressing. The fourteenth chapter of Job is not distressing, nor the *Antigone*, nor even *King Lear*. *The Ruined Cottage* is a simple and pathetic story of misfortune, told in pure English and good verse; but the heavenly alchemy is absent.'

We always know where we are with Housman. Fifteen years earlier he had been exchanging letters with his fellow scholar Gilbert Murray, who had been urging the claims of pacifism and an international morality based on Christian principles. 'I rather doubt', wrote Housman, 'if man really has much to gain by substituting peace for strife, as you and Jesus Christ recommend.'

God is not mocked, as St Paul long ago warned the Galatians. When man gets rid of a great trouble he is easier for a little while, but not for long: Nature instantly sets to work to weaken his power of sustaining trouble, and very soon seven pounds is as heavy as fourteen pounds used to be. Last Easter Monday a young woman threw herself into the Lea because her dress looked so shabby amongst the holiday crowd: in other times and countries women have been ravished by half-a-dozen dragoons and taken it less to heart. It looks to me as if the state of mankind always had been and always would be a state of just tolerable discomfort.

In spite of the offhand tone, the reader does not feel the writer

of the letter is merely being callous about the fate of the young
woman, or that he takes a flippant view of her situation. These
are things that genuinely haunt his imagination, and the
conclusion he draws is one brooded on over a length of years.
(There is the odd further point, not unsuited to Housman's
matter-of-fact view of theology, that God and Jesus Christ
appear to be taking different sides of the question, God being
on Housman's side)

The two passages tell us something about Housman and
about his art, and they have their own sort of logic. None the
less, such comments have made serious persons turn away
from him with impatience, although they may accord respect
to pessimists such as Hardy or Winwood Reade, whose novel
The Martyrdom of Man, published in 1872, itself seems to have
caused a number of suicides. For Reade, as later for
H. G. Wells who much admired the book, and for other
thinkers and men of letters, the truest thought of the century
was Nietzsche's: 'Once upon a time there was a star on which
clever beasts invented knowing . . . That was the most
arrogant and mendacious minute of world history, but
nevertheless it was only a minute.' For Nietzsche man is only
himself when he recognizes his brief independence from a
wholly unfeeling natural order. For Hardy, less logical,
thought itself was to blame: the fault was not nature's but that
of human consciousness:

> But the disease of feeling germed,
> And primal rightness took the tint of wrong;
> Ere nescience shall be reaffirmed
> How long, how long?

Housman gives the impression sometimes of not taking these
sad matters all that seriously. For him the thinkers of the
nineteenth century had not discovered anything that would
have been unfamiliar to poets, generals, and loose-livers in
classical times. High heaven and earth did, and always would,
ail from their prime foundation. Housman himself has his own
kind of trouble, which sets him apart, 'a stranger and
afraid | In a world I never made'. The only alleviation is a
mixture of hedonism and stoicism, the stoicism commended to
the Shropshire Lad by the Grecian statue in a London art
gallery:

> . . . I thought the look would say,
> 'We both were fashioned far away;
> We neither knew, when we were young,
> These Londoners we live among.'

Shropshire is the myth, the view remembered, and the real place; the lad whose identity is made by these things is one set apart. Housman himself was a Worcestershire lad; and his Shropshire, as he once explained in a letter, was 'not exactly a real place'. It was more like 'the Cambridge of Lycidas'. Late in life he replied to a query from an admirer in France that he had never spent much time in Shropshire, and that the details in his poems were 'sometimes quite wrong'. 'I had a sentimental feeling for Shropshire because its hills were our western horizon.'

No more to it than that. The flat and courteous and mildly repressive tone gave nothing away, but probably there was no more to give. There seems to be no secret or hidden pattern in the sequence; but its reality for its readers has produced a number of explanations of *A Shropshire Lad*'s structure and arrangement.* As with Shakespeare's Sonnets, a key and a lock have to be supplied by the customer: the maker did not imagine the need for one, so he can now seem to have worked on a cryptic plan. But there is no plan: only buried instinct and conscious isolation. A Shropshire Lad is two people. He is a native, settled among friends in friendly places, and he is a man on his own. To be the first man—drinking beer, keeping goal, marching to the wicket with bat and pad—is the dream of the second; yet the pair have always been on the closest terms. The man of grief has always tried to be glad. 'Try I will; no harm in trying.'

A certain sort of romanticism has always been concerned with choice, or with the inability to choose. In poetry this generates its own kind of myth, from Keats's 'Do I wake or sleep?' to Larkin's 'Come and choose wrong'. Shropshire is a kingdom of the mythical alternative, a place where 'normal' people lead their heroic and pastoral lives, ending in suicide, enlistment, early death; and where the opposite dream is of such a normality. The second Shropshire Lad ardently desires

---

* For a discussion of these see B. J. Leggett, *Housman's Land of Lost Content* (London, 1970). Leggett's book also includes an excellent and comprehensive bibliography of essays and articles on Housman.

to learn the trade of man and the fate of man born of woman; but he himself is doomed—by choice or by chance—to live solitary as an outsider, 'and die of age and not of pain'.

Some of Housman's dreams depend upon a saving absence of choice. 'On the idle hill of summer' (*ASL*, xxxv) contrasts the life of the second lad, the Shropshire dreamer, with the life and death of those who have enlisted. But 'Woman bore me, I will rise'. Being a man, and notionally the first kind of Shropshire Lad, he must and will get up and join up. The bugle calls; the fifes are screaming like wounded men or women in childbirth; the steady drumming that drowns the voice of water is a noise in dreams, but they are dreams of solidarity with humankind.

Shropshire is both the kingdom of fantasy and the land of wished-for reality. Keats, too, dreamed of mastering human reality, of learning 'the agonies, the strife of human hearts'. When choice is made mythical it can be a myth on both sides and about two lives, one led in sleep and poetry, the other in the open field. Housman's own legend of the soldiery can by the same token mean two things: one illustrated by 'On the idle hill of summer', the other by 'The street sounds to the soldiers' tread' (*ASL*, xxii), the poem in which he exchanges looks with 'a single redcoat'. In the first he is joining up in every sense, with army and with human race. In the second the dream is of a single and unique encounter, the outsider meeting another outsider. Both are dreams.

The general fate that lies in store for the world of humanity and for the universe itself will bring us all together in the end, and rescue us from making the choice of a personal destiny, whether in life or in the myth of poetry. Like a Shropshire fate, or that of a soldier, apocalypse is one of Housman's saving themes. The world will founder before long. The priest in Graham Greene's novel *The Power and the Glory* looks up at the stars and cannot believe this world would shine with the same kind of brilliance. 'It would roll heavily under space in its fog, like a burning and abandoned ship.'

> I wake from dreams and turning
>   My vision on the height
> I scan the beacons burning
>   About the fields of night.

> Each in its stedfast station
> Inflaming heaven they flare;
> They sign with conflagration
> The empty moors of air.

> The signal-fires of warning
> They blaze, but none regard;
> And on through night to morning
> The world runs ruinward.
>
> (*MP*, xliii)

God is not mocked, but the brute and blackguard who made the world will also bring poets metaphors for their poetry. Graham Greene takes as much relish in metaphors of apocalypse as Housman does. There is a silliness in all such metaphors, which is part of their point and their fun. Housman's are better because more unselfconscious. He needed them, as sex made him need war, a far grave in which a soldier sleeps with the bullet in him. All this keeps him happy in his own way, and he was a man who knew how to be happy. He was on the best of terms with grief as well. The spirit of contradiction was always strong in him; even his abuse was a form of intimacy, which is rather more reassuring than not to anyone who admires and tries to write about his poetry.

'I wake from dreams' was not published by Housman; it appeared after his death in the collection edited by his brother Laurence. As with other poems, it may have been finished or revised late in his life, and begun early. He thought it worth keeping, but not worth bringing out himself. As we know from the preface to *More Poems*, Laurence was 'permitted' but not 'enjoined' by his brother 'to publish any poems which appear to him to be completed and to be not inferior to the average of my published poems'. In *A.E.H.*, his memoir of his brother, he printed a few more poems, subsequently included in the collected editions as *Additional Poems*. It is not possible to date poems with any certainty from manuscript sources, and as Christopher Ricks observes in the notes to his *Collected Poems and Selected Prose*, 'the only wise alternative to the present messy morass of MSS in Housman's case will be a full and exact edition of all the poems'. This is now being prepared by Archie Burnett for the Oxford University Press; and his definitive edition is sure to clear up any points that can be cleared up. Invaluable bibliographical work has already been done over the years by John Carter and John Sparrow.

Housman may possibly have omitted 'I wake from dreams' from *Last Poems*, the collection he published in 1922, because its metaphorical structure did not satisfy his taste in the long run. How should men take warning from the signals, and what difference would it make if they did? And yet its many metaphors assemble into an accuracy, like columns scanned in an infallible Bradshaw. The catastrophe it warns of seems to have a timetable predictability, and should have satisfied the textual critic's instinct for getting it right. The paradox itself is steadfast: stars as beacons lit on field or mountain transform themselves into signals winking impassively as the world express hurtles past. The clarity of the images identify with the complexity of their suggestion. Doom arranged from eternity takes on the contingency of a railway accident, with a locomotive running through open country (who but Housman would have put in a poem about star-gazing that phrase 'the empty moors of air'?) and from night into morning. The crash is unavoidable but untimed. 'Ruin', as Owen Barfield pointed out in his book *Poetic Diction*, is a tumultuous word—'heaven ruining from heaven' in *Paradise Lost*—which has become stilled into a motionless one. Both senses collide in Housman's poem, speed with fixity. In his time the image of a train disaster was a haunting one, and the last paradox here is of a world travelling not into the peace of darkness and extinction but into an uncertainty of dawn and danger. The smash will come some time, and might come any time.

When he was 22 Housman contributed to a magazine called *Waifs and Strays* 'New Year's Eve', a poem which imagines the farewell of the old gods in a now godless age, and which was not reprinted until Carter's *Collected Poems* of 1939. Laurence Housman said his brother told him he wrote it at the age of 20 ('I was then a deist'), but left it out of both of his own collections because 'it smacked too much of the Swinburnian style he had abandoned'. Its most striking phrase inverts the proper sentiment 'heaven have mercy on us': 'To-day we are gods, to-morrow | Hell have mercy on us.' Swinburne could have composed that inverted litany; probably Hardy would not have done so, although he might well have composed a very similar poem about the gods' departure. Housman might have written it at any age. It is explosive but demure, and as if absent-minded; for even when young he had acquired the knack of not drawing attention to such things in his poems. Deaths and endings were already routine for him, although their generalized rhetoric will soon begin to summon up something personal.

Additional Poems includes one entitled 'An Epitaph':

> Stay, if you list, O passer by the way;
> Yet night approaches; better not to stay.
>   I never sigh, nor flush, nor knit the brow,
>   Nor grieve to think how ill God made me, now.
> Here, with one balm for many fevers found,
> Whole of an ancient evil, I sleep sound.
>
> (AP, xii)

Housman's own test of poetry—a skin beginning to bristle, and a shivering down the spine—may probably be experienced by the reader half-way through the second line. It is an involuntary sensation, although it must be related in some way to the reader's practice and previous experience. Housman himself implies, without stating it for a fact, that the unwary or ignorant reader is more sensitive to the test.

Whether that is true or not, the effect here comes partly from the poem's use of an old and tried convention. We are urged not to read it, or not to continue reading. Paul Celan used the same convention in his poem 'Engführung', on the victims of Hitler's extermination camps: 'Lies nicht mehr—schau! | Schau nicht mehr—geh!' ('Read no more—look! | Look no more—go!') Those lines also echo a Greek original; and if Housman had read them he would certainly have encountered in himself the physical symptoms he recognized. The symptoms do not seem part of a professional appreciation. Those who read poetry usually do so in the same sense in which regulars visit the theatre, and neither class is necessarily visited by these involuntary shudders. None the less, when Aristotle speaks of pity and terror, and of their purgation, he may have been thinking of symptoms similar to those which Housman describes.

Housman's view is selective and arbitrary. Poetry must 'work' immediately; and his own came to him in accordance with that requirement. He had been influenced, he said, by hymns and Heine, the Border Ballads and Shakespeare's songs; and it was these above all which provoked the physical symptoms. Was it naive of him, or was it a pretence of naviety, to seem to regard such symptoms as definitive? In any age there must be different kinds of poetry, kinds which require other kinds of attention, kinds which do not produce this symptom at all. Was he perverse, philistine, unintelligent—or all three? Some critics suggest that he was, but he would hardly have cared about that. He did not write for the critics; any more, as he once remarked, than the Romans wrote for the benefit of modern classical scholars.

The physical effect, the shiver and the watery eye, must have complex causes. All very well, in 'I wake from dreams', for the starry universe to contemplate the imminent disappearance of earth. Does Housman's art, in Adorno's words, 'provide an implicit critique of the conditions which produced it'? In a sense it does, though perhaps not one that would have satisfied the Marxist theoretician. But a critique, and a very positive one, is certainly there. Paul Celan created, in the age of the Holocaust, a 'critique' which makes the term a classic understatement. 'Look no more—go!' Housman's is, in its own way, just as absolute. The poetry he instinctively turned to is especially capable of such positive refusals and negative demands. Taken by itself, Milton's line 'Nymphs and shepherds, dance no more' moved him to tears.

Classical epitaphs, like that of Simonides on the men who died at Thermopylae, contain by custom an injunction to the reader. The one in Celan's poem is like a scream unheard in a silence, the eternally empty silence in the area of memorial. Housman's second line has its own kind of silence, which makes the third sound relaxed and judicious, even chatty: at which point the reader becomes aware that such a tone was not, after all, so absent in the second line. The still everyday phrase 'Better not to . . .' ('Better not to leave the car on a yellow line') here gets its power to shiver the spine from the unexpected association of grave warning with relaxed familiarity. But that note of familiarity in the second does not make the third line any less of a surprise; as if another poem, and a quite different one, started here.

Possibly Housman thought so too, and left the poem alone because it might seem to give something away. According to R. P. Graves's biography, *A. E. Housman: The Scholar-Poet*, it may have been written as early as 1886, ten years before the publication of *A Shropshire Lad*. The manuscript is in Notebook A, the earliest, which also has a line or two of fragments that sound related: 'Day falls, night climbs, the hour has lost its name . . . And here you loiter spelling gravestones: go.' But these fragments do not suggest anything of the contrast between form and personality which makes the whole poem come as close as any of Housman's to revealing his special sorts of poetic effect. It is a contrast between what is appropriate to a classical epitaph, and something that suggests the author's own sense of himself. The speaker begins as a familiar figure, uttering the sentiment that night comes— *nox venit*—and this 'passer by the way' could be a figure from Greek translation, even a cousin of that 'head of a traveller' from the author's youthful joke 'Fragment of a Greek Tragedy'. The prickle of terror in the advice of that second line has at least part of its source in a conventional, if concealed, irony. A man secure in the night of death reminds the traveller of the dangers in the night that falls every day of his life. He must pay a proper care to those, even while being reminded of the other night to come.

The speaker of the first two lines is conventionally anonymous. The 'I' who breaks in at line three might almost be another and a different person, who bursts into confidences long withheld, stored up in the grave's isolation. In its few lines the poem hints at a whole dimension of confessional monologue, which the dead man would now be free to indulge, if it were possible for him to do so. The speaker of the third and fourth lines could be still alive, reminiscing; content, if not almost complacent, in his sense of healing time. The sigh of a mourner becomes that of a former lover, ironized by the unexpected 'flush'. The word recalls moments in Keats— 'Ethereal, flush'd, and like a throbbing star'—where the sexual sense is barely concealed by the diction. The inspired awkwardness in Keats's poetic use brings it close to what in

life can be a comfortless yearning, which is the feeling hidden
in the centre of Housman's lines.

Young men flush or blush, and hate doing it, as an
involuntary symptom which cannot be hidden. In *A.E.H.*,
Laurence Housman says that his brother, when asked about
his refusal of the Order of Merit, 'suddenly blushed . . . (an
unexpected gift which he had retained from the days of his
youth)'. We may suspect it was a 'gift' which the young man
would have preferred to do without. Young men flush in love,
and in the presence of the beloved, particularly if their passion
is unrequited. In solitude, misery and disgust expresses itself
in a grimace. Grieving, alliterated here with God, is a physical
display of emotion. In 'The Funeral of Youth: Threnody', a
poem written twenty years or so later than Housman's,
Rupert Brooke personifies the mourners, one of whom is
'*Grief*, so noisy a widow, that all said, | "Had he but wed | Her
elder sister *Sorrow*, in her stead!"' The sound of the two words
may have come to imply a distinction in the sense. Sorrow
would be compatible with the silent 'now' which ends the
fourth line.

After the suddenly intimate and confidential note of the two
lines inset, the speaker returns to something more like the
convention in which he began. This is without any doubt the
dead addressing the living: a grave doctor recommending a
universal panacea. Like other doctors, he does not explicitly
claim the remedy as his own invention, but he has personal
knowledge that it works. In using the topos of advice or
instruction addressed by the dead to the living, Wordsworth,
and at a later date Walter de la Mare, showed a special
aptitude for the convention. Conversely, critics interested in
the same convention, like Paul de Man and Jonathan Culler,
have analysed its effects theoretically. Keats's fragment
beginning; 'This living hand, now warm and capable . . .' has
particular interests for these theorists, because Keats as living
poet is affecting to address his living reader as if from beyond
the grave. His tone is the warning or exhortatory one of
epitaphs; but not here telling the reader what to expect.
Instead, it requires from him a sacrifice of his own hand, to
replace that of the poet at a time when the latter will be in his
grave. Were he to make such a sacrifice the reader might feel
better, be 'conscience calmed'.

But of course Keats's reader can't do it, even prospectively, and the unreasonableness of the demand adds to its pathos. In the second version of 'Hyperion', Keats refers to the time 'when this warm scribe, my hand, is in the grave'; and 'warm' has something of the same impact as 'flush' in Housman's lines. Keats projects the warmth of his body forward into death. Housman's speaker recalls it as the symptom of an illness now cured and past. Both give the impression of life and death as possibly continuous states, transformed into poetry in the present.

But Keats has a sick man's longing for the health of others, and a resentment that such health cannot be bequeathed by them to him. Housman's speaker, who also seems to address us from both death and life, is enjoying repose and remission from life's fevers. The word 'flush' here suggests life and vigour more strongly than it suggests sickness. And although sound sleep is attributed to the grave, it is really a sign of health among the living. The last two lines double this life-and-death irony, for the speaker has never admitted to being dead, but only to being relieved from fret and fever. And though he is now 'whole of an ancient evil', such a wholeness is far from being true of the poem itself. It is packed with discrepant effects, some of which, as in the second line, make the reader's hair stand up.

The poem evades, or displaces, all the formulae in it. It avoids the working-out of a continuous conceit, or demonstrating its point symmetrically. Its varied tones of communication are by no means all compatible with each other: but they unite in an obscure satisfaction and superiority, which also seem sardonically conscious of their own attitude. The pathos of Keats's proleptic plea as epitaph has no parallel in Housman. His dead man is not asking for anything, nor recommending a remedy to others; but his words vividly suggest that the warmth of life, with all its attendant anguish and embarrassment, is what the living have, and he does not. He professes to be well away from it all, and indifferent to the reader who is not; but the third and fourth lines are his own sort of confession that he would rather be alive than dead. The blend of ceremonious formality with secrecy, a hidden intimacy, is typical of Housman, and as moving in its own way as Keats's openness.

And it is a blend which keeps. We have all had the experience of being struck by a poem, even given shivers by it, only to find the potency diminished with time, perhaps gone entirely. John Crowe Ransom's epitaph 'Here lies a Lady' has a style and manner that immediately compel the reader, but do not last. One reason may be that Ransom's style has to be 'whole', and uniform, to work as it does; like fine play, it cannot outlive the match. The durability of Housman's poems, which may increasingly be recognized by a new generation of formalists and of poets concerned with the uses of regularity, depends on combinations of factors which come with time to seem increasingly complex. What gives a shiver in 'An Epitaph' is not only the strange mixture of pathos with what is pleased and sardonic, but a touch of irony, even of parody, in the self-presentation. Personality is present, not as style but in addition to style.

Housman, it appears, sometimes 'dreamed' short poems, or bits of poems. One of them is reported by his brother as the famous four lines beginning: 'When the bells justle in the tower | The hollow night amid', lines which were particularly admired by W. H. Auden, and which I shall return to later. He is also said to have dreamed this couplet:

> Above the soldier's grave there twine
> The Woodbine and the Concubine.

Deadpan, like much of his verse, it suggests a striking mixture of studied elegance and secret hilarity. Concubine is a beautiful word, and so is woodbine: their entwining together is startling, like much that arrests the eye in Housman's pages, and mingles in a sort of brisk languor the pastoral and military, classic and commercial, making a miniature elegy of the whole. Dream consciousness appears to transpose two heraldic flowers, turning woodbine into its other sense of a cheap tobacco favoured by the military, and making a columbine out of a camp-follower. The two form a poetic stele in relief, with elements from a classic and an early Romantic pictorial context, flower-crowned urns and stencils on cigarette packets. The punning transpositions give the couplet its curious charm, while drawing no direct attention to themselves.

If Housman could dream a kind of self-parody, he could also assume a different identity in the same context. Another set of his dream verses suggest G. K. Chesterton, beginning

> When I was born in a world of sin,
> Praise be God it was raining gin.

Possibly Housman did not care greatly for Chesterton's personality or works, although he seems to have quite liked *The Ballad of the White Horse*, but his dream self (he was apparently conscious of his Chestertonian persona) unerringly hits off the most irritating feature of that author's light verse: the bluff but coy attention it draws to its own whimsicalities. His own verse draws no such attention, whether composed waking or in dream. But he is certainly capable of too great an obviousness, or a jauntiness not set off by the blank, tight tones which seem to go with unsmiling features. 'Oh is it the jar of nations' (*AP*, xiv) is an example, a rejected poem that might well have been written with Hardy in mind, or in sympathy with him: for Hardy, unlike Chesterton, was clearly a poet for whom Housman felt a respect which was as evidently returned. Hardy's favourite poem from *A Shropshire Lad* was 'Is my team ploughing?' (xxvii). 'Oh is it the jar of nations' belongs to the same genre, a colloquy between the dead and the living, itself a variant of the voice as epitaph. Hardy's manner in such a poem is more relaxed; and there is an important difference, to be discussed later, between the purposes for which the two poets use the genre. 'Is my team ploughing?' certainly brings the Housman shiver, particularly in its last verse, and that is not something which Hardy's poetry needs to do, or which Hardy himself made any special point about. But the first stanza of this poem is almost exactly in Hardy's vein 'on the breaking of nations':

> 'Oh is it the jar of nations,
>   The noise of a world run mad,
> The fleeing of earth's foundations?'
>   Yes, yes; lie quiet, my lad.

The dead man thinks his country is calling him, and longs to take part in her new perils. ' "Oh is it the newsboys crying | Lost battle, retreat, despair, | And honour and

England dying?"' The poet reassures him that, although it is
so, there is nothing he can do about it. The concluding verse
has the unassuming flatness of some of Hardy's similar poems:

> The devil this side of the darnels
> Is having a dance with man,
> And quarrelsome chaps in charnels
> Must bear it as best they can.

'Chaps' and 'lads' would not be unsuited to Hardy, but he
would make the dialogue more in the nature of things. He
might have used the rhyme ('darnel' is a country term for
coarse grass), but would have made the upshot of the idea
more wondering. As his poem 'Channel Firing' shows, Hardy
is more taken with a specific locality, and with the identity of
those taking part. Housman has no equivalent of Parson
Thirdly, or 'starlit Stonehenge'.

Although the conjuration of the dead, and of dead soldiers,
was vital to Housman's muse, he may have rejected poems too
obvious in their emotion, or too lacking in his own kind of fun:

> 'Tis five years since, 'An end,' said I;
> 'I'll march no further, time to die.
> All's lost; no worse has heaven to give.'
> Worse it has given, and yet I live.
>
> (*AP*, xv)

The poem grinds on its way brilliantly, but too steadily, as if
the reference to thoughts of suicide 'five years since' had made
the author cautious to the point of woodenness. That is the
penalty Housman sometimes pays for being (apparently) too
forthcoming and telling the reader

> I shall not die to-day, no fear:
> I shall live yet for many a year,
> And see worse ills and worse again,
> And die of age and not of pain.

That turned out to be prophetic enough, but the tone seems
subtly wrong. *King Lear* may not be distressing, but a
borrowing from it here ('The worst is not so long as we can say
"This is the worst"') removes despair on to an altogether too-
literary plane. Nor are matters mended by the measured

ingenuity which follows, recounting God's attempts to prop
up the heavens with steel, basalt, or diamond:

> What found he, that the heavens stand fast?
> What pillar proven firm at last
> Bears up so light that world-seen span?
> The heart of man, the heart of man.

The heart of man is not really Housman's thing; and the
solemn note, appropriate to the climax of the pseudo-hymn
into which the poem has turned, here marks one of his few
failures in the art of near parody. A blend of the personal with
stoic doxology has failed to come off.

That may be why the poem remained unpublished. 'The
chestnut casts his flambeaux' (*LP*, ix), begun in 1896, the year
of the publication of *A Shropshire Lad*, does the heavy act much
more successfully, the last stanza only being completed in
time for its publication in *Last Poems* in 1922.

> The troubles of our proud and angry dust
>   Are from eternity, and shall not fail.
> Bear them we can, and if we can we must.
>   Shoulder the sky, my lad, and drink your ale.

The note of the poem has been both weighty and deadpan
from its opening ('The chestnut casts his flambeaux, and the
flowers | Stream from the hawthorn on the wind away'). The
poet's eye has been not so much on human ills as on the words
and gestures that poets and men use to convey a response to
them. The heavy hand in the verse is lightened by its own
sense of what it is up to, giving a wink to the ale-drinking lad
whose proud and angry dust is always in trouble of some sort.

If Housman's varieties and mutations of tone are often
based on parody, of himself and others, of hymns or ballads,
they drive home, perhaps for that reason, a strong sense of his
integrity. Every note he adopts, in language or sentiment, has
the usual effect of making him more completely himself. But
the poems he rejected for publication during his lifetime may
show ways in which he did not choose to make a public
appearance, as they may also show his dissatisfaction with the
working out of poetic structures. Some of those he rejected,
like 'An Epitaph', may possibly have been omitted for both

reasons. But that is why they are of importance in understanding the ways his poetry works. Although his poems can
be brilliant in the ways in which they draw attention to
themselves, his very best effects are always unobtrusive.

They can also be, in the most obvious sense, 'non-poetical',
because seeming to be uttered involuntarily and on the spur of
the moment, as if they were exclamations like 'Look out!' or
'Can I help you?' Even such an opening as 'From far, from eve
and morning', with its poetical 'eve' in the middle, sounds as
spontaneous as 'Oh, when I was in love with you', or 'Stars, I
have seen them fall'. These urgent openings, addressed as well
to the dead as to the living, come naturally together with the
endings, making each an epitaph or farewell as well as a cry of
recognition. Housman's most perfectly underplayed opening
is the first line of 'To an Athlete Dying Young':

> The time you won your town the race
> We chaired you through the market-place;
> Man and boy stood cheering by,
> And home we brought you shoulder-high.
>
> (*ASL*, xix)

'Chairing' and 'cheering' seem adventitiously felicitous neigh-
bours, but the real effect is in the first line, and the definite
article which is the first word. ('That time' would have
overstressed the commonplace, and spoilt the poem's quiet
absorption in the memory.) The simplicity of remembering
contrasts with the consignment of farewell, parting with him
to another crowd, when the dead runner seems to enter
another sort of erotic perpetuity:

> And round that early-laurelled head
> Will flock to gaze the strengthless dead,
> And find unwithered on its curls
> The garland briefer than a girl's.

In 'To An Athlete Dying Young', the living man addresses the
speechless dead. In the epitaph 'Stay, if you list' the dead man
buttonholes the living, with a pretence of not caring whether
or not he listens. 'Is my team ploughing?' enacts the
homeliness (no wonder Hardy liked it) of an exchange
between hearty, rather embarrassed young man and frail,
wistful invalid, avid for news but secretly hoping the world

has not been able to get along without him. Dialogue dramatizes the difference between jealousy in the dead or done for, and the insensitivity of the living and the strong. The speaker in 'An Epitaph' strove, not altogether successfully, to seem pleased with being dead. But the dead ploughman does not pretend to be wise and knowing; he is longing for news but afraid to ask. It is the living man who advises him not to stay and ask a further question.

CHAPTER 2

Love

> He would not stay for me; and who can wonder?
> He would not stay for me to stand and gaze.
> I shook his hand and tore my heart in sunder
> And went with half my life about my ways.
>
> <div align="right">(<i>AP</i>, vii)</div>

Referring, as it undoubtedly does, to Housman's strong and
single love for his friend Moses Jackson, first met when both
were Oxford undergraduates, the verse ends with an archaic
phrase of self-deprecation. But in terms of his poetry's effects,
their decision and accuracy, that fourth line is something of a
verbal *tour de force*, combining as it does a slightly prissy
archaism with the grim clinical precision of 'half my life'. The
contrast has even greater symmetry in the previous line,
where the separate acts of shaking the hand and tearing the
heart appear synonymous, blended into one. All the writer
wishes to do is to stand and gaze, like a lover; but the object of
devotion exhibits a scriptural impatience, and like jesting
Pilate will not stay to answer what is in this case an
unspoken question. There is no reproach in this, although
standing and staying ('They stood, and earth's foundations
stay') has an important role in Housman's emotional icono-
graphy. The loved one will not stay for the writer: he must do
his staying elsewhere. The precise syllables of the fourth line
pick their way through the ensuing wilderness with their own
kind of stoic fidelity:

> If death and time are stronger,
> A love may yet be strong;
> The world will last for longer,
> But this will last for long.
>
> <div align="right">(<i>AP</i>, ix)</div>

This is a variant, probably an earlier one, of the more robust
and finished version of the argument which Laurence Housman
printed in *More Poems*:

I promise nothing: friends will part;
   All things may end, for all began;
And truth and singleness of heart
   Are mortal even as is man.

But this unlucky love should last
   When answered passions thin to air;
Eternal fate so deep has cast
   Its sure foundation of despair.
                         (*MP*, xii)

The tone of the poem is full of a kind of humour, audible only in the intonation of certain words and phrases. The tone is that of a family solicitor (Housman's father was one) putting the tips of his fingers together as he reassures a client. He can't promise anything, but—yes—the contract should be honoured, and the arrangement be made permanent. There is not only buried humour in the verses but a buried logic, whose implications are equally droll. Since there is no opposite party in this contract, it follows that the arrangement is the more likely to be a secure one. There is nothing to disturb it.

Influence is an ambiguous matter in Housman's verse, and sometimes very far indeed from the Bible or Burns, Shakespeare's songs or the Ballad. The theme of love can take a more subterraneous route:

Ask me no more, for fear I should reply;
   Others have held their tongues, and so can I;
Hundreds have died, and told no tale before:
   Ask me no more, for fear I should reply—

How one was true and one was clean of stain
   And one was braver than the heavens are high,
And one was fond of me: and all are slain.
   Ask me no more, for fear I should reply.
                         (*AP*, vi)

To a motif based on the form of a vilanelle the poet brings a query, itself based on classical rhetoric, that echoes a Caroline lyric; but the more immediate model is from Tennyson's medley *The Princess*. Carew's rhetorical love poem 'Ask me no more where Jove bestows | When June is past, the fading rose', pretends a question, and answers it with a succession of conceits. Housman alters the rhythm, and adds, with a further

alteration of tone, a sardonic rider. His rhetorical figure is an
occupatio—the announcement that a topic will not be discussed, which includes the discussion of it—but he turns this,
together with both his other models, into the reversal of a
third type: the recounting of a heroic deed. Poems about
heroes are also about their heroic ends, and this is the subject
of refusal. Horace says that there were many strong men
before Agamemnon, but their names are unrecorded.
Housman's heroes have all the virtues by implication, but like
Arthurian knights are chiefly famous for one. The fourth to be
unsung is famous because he was fond of the poet, who now
declines to compose the song. After his three peers, this fourth
man's source of fame is itself ironic: he did not love the poet;
he was fond of him; and this may be a classic understatement
or litotes, or it may be the plain, unvarnished truth. In any
event it marks the climax of a poem which three times declines
to begin. No heroic tale is to be told, although the poet
concludes by warning his audience that he may yet tell it, if he
is importuned long enough.

'How one was clean of stain' suggests Housman's own
translation of Horace's ode *Diffugere Nives* (Book 4, no. 7),
which he once spoke of before a class as the most 'beautiful' of
all Latin poems. His translation, itself beautifully crafted,
naturally makes no ploys or quietly secret games, like that in
'Ask me no more'. The last stanza of the ode commemorates a
hero who died by violence, and two more whom fate separated
at the last:

> Night holds Hippolytus the pure of stain,
>   Diana steads him nothing, he must stay;
> And Theseus leaves Pirithoüs in the chain
>   The love of comrades cannot take away.
>   (*MP*, v)

Diana cannot aid her virgin protégé, and the reckless courage
of the famous pair has ended in disaster; Horace of course
makes no mention of any heroic figure who was 'fond of' the
poet. But as we shall see later, Housman expands and changes
Horace's ending in his own poem 'Hell Gate', which is about
two soldier comrades who escape together from the dark lord's
dominion. Theseus and Pirithoüs went to hell to carry off

Pluto's queen, Persephone. In one version of the tale Pluto lets
Theseus go; in another he is rescued by Heracles. But
Pirithoüs remained in confinement, and according to one
source of the legend in a stone block which grew into his body.
Housman knew this, and knew himself a man into whom the
stone or iron had entered. 'Ask me no more' implies such
things by its silence, by its refusal to recount them: 'Others
have held their tongues, and so can I.'

Some of his lines appear to lie in wait for the reader, rather
as if they were the comments on delinquent scholars which in
his later years he seems to have stored up for future use.
Where there is no suggestion of something in this kind in
reserve, poems of this type may remain inert, their torsion and
tensity no more than decorative:

> Oh on my breast in days hereafter
>   Light the earth should lie,
> Such weight to bear is now the air,
>   So heavy hangs the sky.
>
> (*AP*, x)

Such a verse has no power of startling the reader with a
hidden communication, the power that Housman secretly and
passionately valued. Bright or ingenious ideas, of the sort that
are so comfortably communal in metaphysical poetry, tend to
have the reverse effect with him. The conceit about the heavy
air seems not to move him with the wish to share it, as it
would with Donne or Herbert, nor to incite further creativity
in the same vein. But this is certainly not true of another four-
line verse in *Additional Poems*, where the idea seems to burst out
into involuntary emotion.

> Now to her lap the incestuous earth
>   The son she bore has ta'en.
> And other sons she brings to birth
>   But not my friend again.
>
> (*AP*, viii)

This, although low-toned, is violent; and while the violence is
not directed at the reader it is involved in the need to
communicate with him. The first line seems a pent-up whisper
of resentment, now released into the reader's ear. 'Incestuous'
has the same sound and note of spoken drama that it bears in

Hamlet, and the elided 'ta'en' suggests some similar context in the conversation of drama. But the message, though intense, is characteristically cool. Earth couples with her dead son, and the thought is torment to his jealous lover, the speaker in the poem. It is a literal love torment, far removed from that clever, gloomy satisfaction in the thought that the weight of the earth in the grave will be less than that of the sky when one is living. In the harsh and slow reluctance of these lines there is none the less something tender. The earth mother's embrace (the manuscript has 'lap' above an uncancelled 'bed') is also the consolation and repose of the death in which she cradles him. 'Incestuous' is a bitter word, but the speaker knows that the lap or bed of earth is a place of satisfaction for her son, his friend, whether as adult or as child.

Housman's figures and conceits are not usually Shakespearean, which is natural enough in a poet who seemed inclined to agree with Samuel Johnson that Shakespeare nowhere wrote more than half-a-dozen consecutive lines of good poetry. Shakespearean image and metaphor generates itself in the heat of utterance, often by short circuits in the sense and association of words, and Housman's language is not a bit like that. There is a big difference between the spontaneous ease of Shakespeare and the more mysterious ease (poetry, he once wrote, was 'either easy or impossible' for him) with which his verse came to Housman. Even when, as in this four-line poem, there is a touch of Shakespeare's dramatic tone, it has been subdued by the precision of the process by which Housman revised his first inspiration.

At the same time the lines *are* a kind of outburst, and one in which resentment and tenderness meet in the hollowness of grief. The elements of a funerary conceit can rarely have been used with such complex feeling. In the last line all jealousy of the incestuous mother is forgotten, as is resentment of her unmeaning fecundity. The friend who is dead remains. Housman's friend Moses Jackson ('Oxford had not much effect on me, except that I there met my greatest friend') died in Vancouver in 1925. Previously he had been headmaster of a school in India, and he and Housman had not met for many years. Jackson's last letter to him, in pencil, was inked over by Housman to preserve the writing. At the time of Jackson's wedding he had composed, or had begun to compose, an 'Epithalamium', which was completed in 1922 and published that year in *Last Poems*. In his biography of the poet, Norman Page suggested that Housman consented to collect and publish *Last Poems* as an offering to his friend, whom he knew by then to be seriously ill. This seems quite possible, and it is also reported—the letter is in private hands—that Housman told his friend at the time, 'you are largely responsible for my writing poetry'.

In his memoir, Laurence Housman opined that 'Ask me no more' had been set aside by Housman 'because he had used a refrain made familiar in one of Tennyson's lyrics'. That does not explain why he should have used it, although Laurence Housman was no doubt right in thinking his brother had no wish to see the poem in print. The relation of 'Ask me no more' to Tennyson's enchanting lyric was certainly an intimate one:

> Ask me no more: the moon may draw the sea;
>   The cloud may stoop from heaven and take the shape
>   With fold to fold, of mountain or of cape;
> But O too fond, when have I answered thee?
>   Ask me no more.
>
> Ask me no more: what answer should I give?
>   I love not hollow cheek or faded eye;
>   Yet, O my friend, I will not have thee die!
> Ask me no more, lest I should bid thee live;
>   Ask me no more.
>
> Ask me no more: thy fate and mine are sealed:
>   I strove against the stream and all in vain:
>   Let the great river take me to the main:
> No more, dear love, for at a touch I yield;
>   Ask me no more.

Housman must have known the poem well. Certainly he must have felt what it meant, and enjoyed in his own inner way the inner drama of love and reluctance Tennyson had put into it, a drama more close and devious than the stilted charade of the poem's story. 'Thy fate and mine are sealed'—that was certainly what he felt about himself and Moses Jackson; and there must for him have been an added poignancy in the speaker of the poem growing more tender with each refusal she gives. 'No more, dear love, for at a touch I yield': it is not hard to think how much that would have affected the poet who took up the Tennysonian refrain which haunted him, and to whom the words 'fond' and 'friend' meant so much.

Jackson might well have said 'But O too fond, when have I answered thee?', if young men of the 1880s had been in the habit of saying such things in affectionate friendship. His friendliness to Housman seems, indeed, to have been of the kind that would not have him die: that, on the contrary, did its cordial best to maintain a close relation while they lived in the same house and worked at the same office. Jackson eventually left London for India, but he never spurned the friendship, or broke it off. Housman's love none the less had to remain unspoken, and poetry—his own or that of others—had to remain its form of speech. Reticence was not only the price of love but the seal of it. Tennyson, we remember, vigorously repudiated any suggestion that he ever called Hallam by any of the endearments that appear in *In Memoriam*. Yet with its fantasy of college emotions and transferences, and of impatience with the always powerful and unadmitted passions, *The Princess* was not only of Tennyson's time, but of his own time for Housman too. A passage that comes soon after the melody 'Ask me no more', all-too clearly defined his own situation after the moment he fell in love:

> But sadness on the soul of Ida fell,
> And hatred of her weakness, blent with shame.
> Old studies failed; seldom she spoke: but oft
> Clomb to the roofs, and gazed alone for hours
> On that disastrous leaguer, swarms of men
> Darkening her female field: void was her use,
> And she as one that climbs a peak to gaze
> O'er land and main, and sees a great black cloud
> Drag inward from the deeps, a wall of night,
> Blot out the slope of sea from verge to shore,
> And suck the blinding splendour from the sand,
> And quenching lake by lake and tarn by tarn
> Expunge the world: so fared she gazing there;
> So blackened all her world in secret, blank
> And waste it seemed and vain.

Old studies did not fail for Housman: on the contrary, in time

they saved. But they certainly failed him when he had shared
digs opposite the college with Moses Jackson; and Housman
too had failed, literally, in his final exams. His world too had
blackened in secret, overarched by a black cloud. But his own
breed of trench humour, too, must have come to life and come
to his aid: his own inner sense of what was comical in his
situation might well have responded here to Tennyson's
equally peculiar fantasy. Tennyson entered into the spirit of
his heroine, who saw swarms of men darkening her female
field. Housman's temperament, as now revealed to him, was
as hostile to normality as the Princess thought her own was.
And all this could be matter for a buried joke: the joke, as he
put it in his own distinctly joking terms, of 'whatever brute
and blackguard made the world'.

The most famous song in *The Princess*, 'Tears, idle tears', is a
part of the Princess's own sad joke about 'haunting the
moulder'd lodges of the past'. For the past is a country in
which to live is to be dead. Tennyson's song becomes ever
more exact and emphatic as it reaches its end:

> deep as love,
> Deep as first love, and wild with all regret;
> O Death in Life, the days that are no more.

Housman must have responded to that lack of mere sentiment,
that unexpected precision.

> Into my heart an air that kills
> From yon far country blows:

In romantic poetry the truths are often also the illusions, the
two lying close together. First love has its real being less in the
moment it occurred than in the death in life which followed it;
and first love was for Housman the only kind. Anyone, he
said, who was always falling in love did not know the meaning
of the word.

This traditional romantic conviction goes with the unalter-
able nature of romantic loss. The air that blows from the far
country and the 'blue remembered hills' destroys because it
brings the death of living in the past. But of course it suited
Housman very well do that emotionally, as it suited him to
live from day to day in what he spoke of as his 'proper job', the

meticulous study of the classics. Like our contemporary, the poet Philip Larkin, Housman illustrates the rare case of the romantic poet who does very well out of his romanticism: not in the sense that it inspires him with poetry, although incidentally it does that too, but because coming to terms with it enabled him to live the kind of life he needed and wanted to live. Both poets would have despised the modern fad among poets, itself a legacy from romantic doctrine, that to the poet and his art all is permitted; that if he loves he can and should destroy and waste others through the fulfilment of his love. The romantic life and its excesses were as alien to both poets as the idea of romantic love was congenial to them.

Reticence for them is therefore a natural and inevitable part of loving, however much this may seem to go against the instinct of the poetry it inspires. But 'others have held their tongues, and so can I'. The classics themselves reinforced the point. '*Vixere fortes ante Agamemnona* . . .', 'Hundreds have died, and told no tale before'. The convention in Housman's reticence identifies with those; and the authority of his poems can seem that of a sudden and secret communication, to one reader alone. His admirers probably all have their favourite examples in which this happens. If it does not take place the poem may be admired for other reasons, but the person in it may not appear the same: he may seem distant, uncongenial, or even false. Intimacy goes on and off, although its absence can be as striking as its presence.

And when he speaks out the poet might still have preferred to hold his tongue, or have spoken as impersonally as a modern oracle. Eliot also spoke like this sometimes, and by doing so accentuated the impression of a strong and personal feeling: 'And I Tiresias have foresuffered all . . .' In Housman the oracular tone can suddenly crumble and vanish before we are aware, in such a phrase as 'And one was fond of me . . .' By implication, and in fact, that 'one' never spoke of it. For Housman, and in his poetry, such a consummation could only come in the presence of death—'the sweetheart he chose'. And yet a kind of wry if ghostly consummation does figure in 'Ask me no more', as it figures throughout his mythology; in what Larkin called 'the haunting, half-realised legend of ploughing, enlisting, betrothals and betrayings and hangings . . .

summertime on Bredon, the wind of Wenlock Edge, and nettles blowing on graves'.

It is possible, none the less, to wonder whether with all his problems, his hopeless love, and his feelings of isolation, Housman would contrive to be as comparatively happy in our world today as he was in that of his own time. It certainly suited him, as it was suited to the kind of life he wished to lead, that he was not by nature a rebellious man. Like that of other and later romantics—Auden, Betjeman, Larkin himself—his poetry is in its own way thrillingly subversive, but it never preaches revolt. On the contrary, it offers its own kind of comfort as a substitute—possibly a deliberate one—for religious comfort. His poetry is certainly not religious in the way that T. S. Eliot thought Baudelaire's *Fleurs du Mal* was. Christopher Ricks has stressed the idea of Housman as a poet whose blasphemy was deliberate, noting that Eliot saw an 'essential congruity' between 'the finest religious verse and the most brilliant blasphemous verse'. If that is the case, it does not apply to Housman, even though Ricks claims that 'Eliot's words in 1927 have their applicability to the poet . . . who published *Last Poems* five years before'.

What is certainly true is the poems' assertion of non-survival as a positive creed, and a consolation to live and die by. Death is the good shepherd; like first love itself, life is a flowering annual, and the dead are best commemorated by flowers whose span is just as brief.

> —Oh, bring from hill and stream and plain
> Whatever will not flower again,
> To give him comfort: he and those
> Shall bide eternal bedfellows . . .
>
> (*ASL*, xlvi)

What is true of a single grave is also true for a whole dead populace; 'the put to death, the perished nation' are the blest of a new, secular mythology. In the demure little hymn, three verses and one sentence, that Housman composed for his own funeral service, the point is made in the same way that he had made it as a young man in the little poem, 'Parta Quies', in memory of his mother. The last verse of 'For my Funeral'

imagines the congregation addressing God in the first-person
plural:

> We now to peace and darkness
> And earth and thee restore
> Thy creature that thou madest
> And wilt cast forth no more.
>
> (*MP*, vlvii)

That is as moving in its own way as Newman's hymn: 'And
with the morn those angel faces smile | Which I have loved
long since, and lost awhile.' Housman did not seem to despise
Christian belief. He gave its traditional language another kind
of hope, and a different authority.

And in a sense a different kind of love. That 'we' is not
insignificant. Housman wanted love, not only the love of one
man, which he could never have, but the solidarity with his
kind that comes from lying in peace and darkness with them
in the grave. To that peace they can restore him, and he can
feel in anticipation their solicitude, which his solitariness
mostly missed in life. They will be fellow-townsmen.

> The time you won your town the race
> We chaired you through the market-place;
> Man and boy stood cheering by,
> And home we brought you shoulder-high.
>
> To-day, the road all runners come,
> Shoulder-high we bring you home,
> And set you at your threshold down,
> Townsman of a stiller town.
>
> (*ASL*, xix)

In 'To an Athlete Dying Young' there is an almost wistful
sense of solidarity with the runner, in life and in death. The
smart lad who slips betimes away is a moving image of all
youthful endeavour, local or in general. 'Smart lad' is swiftly
colloquial, and so is the term 'cut':

> Eyes the shady night has shut
> Cannot see the record cut,

In one of his last letters, to an American admirer who hoped
to write a book about him, Housman explained the term:
'When an athletic performance, previously the best, is

excelled, the *record* is said to be *broken* or *cut*. I am not sure if the
latter is really good English, but it was common in sporting
circles in my youth.' It is certainly a very resonant word in
this poem, suggesting slipping away ('Smart lad, to slip
betimes away | From fields where glory does not stay') as well
as achievement; and bringing present into the classic past
where inscriptions were carved to commemorate both game
and funeral. Emotion in the poem has things both ways too: to
win amongst one's peers is as desirable as to get away on one's
own. Solitude and solidarity merge in the same harmony, as
do even the sexes.

> So set, before its echoes fade,
> The fleet foot on the sill of shade,
> And hold to the low lintel up
> The still-defended challenge-cup.
>
> And round that early-laurelled head
> Will flock to gaze the strengthless dead,
> And find unwithered on its curls
> A garland briefer than a girl's.

It is the other sex which has, in a sense, the last word, the last
gracefulness, one that the sound of the second line in the
penultimate stanza already suggests; and it too merges in its
own harmony with male competition. For war heroes, in
Wilfred Owen's sonnet, 'the pallor of girls' brows shall be
their pall'. Images of devotion flock to Housman's ending, as
do Homer's strengthless dead, equated with we helpless ones
who could never run a mile or cut a record. But fellow-feeling,
absence of exclusion, are as strong in the poem as the love
uniting affection and sorrow.

Moses Jackson went in for and won challenge-cups, and
Housman may have watched him win them: but love in the
poem, although touchingly evident, is as finely generalized as
it is in Wilfred Owen's best poems. Both Eros and Agape can
have in their created world a universal appeal; and his sexual
orientation is in one sense as unimportant in Housman's
mythology as it is in Blake's. Yet it does much to determine
the depth and complexity of his poetic being: the personality
of his poetry, and the individual nature of his romanticism,
come to light in the ways it declares itself. The emotion and

power of love may be general and clear; but in the most successful art sex is usually metamorphosed into the individuality itself, the one man writing. That is certainly true with Housman. In the same way Auden's love poem, 'Lay your sleeping head', might have been written to or about anyone, of either sex. The point is that it has been written by Auden.

CHAPTER 3

Sex and the Soldier

When Housman went for a walk and a bit of a poem came into his head, it arrived as a means of communication with the outside world, a way of getting in touch. And it is striking with what speed and success the lines from the void achieve this intimacy. Naturally enough, perhaps, because they came out of the depths of his being. But not always. Even when the message is in one sense his own, Housman does not always seem himself when giving it. 'Parta Quies', in memory of his mother, written and published in a magazine when he was 22, has, as we have seen, the same message as those three stanzas in one sentence which he wrote for his own funeral. But it is not exactly a personal message, even when it is much more terse.

> Some can gaze and not be sick,
> But I could never learn the trick.
> There's this to say for blood and breath,
> They give a man a taste for death.
>
> (AP, xvi)

This may sound like him, or does it? It is not the man himself, but Housman imitating Housman, as Yeats imitated and remade the personae of Yeats. As with 'Parta Quies' and 'For my Funeral', he is taking what amounts to an official line. The difference is often slight but usually unmistakable. Things that 'give a man' something or other have rather too much of what is generically man-to-man about them. 'There's this to say' sounds confidential, but is the kind of thing one would rather not hear from the kind of person who would say it. Housman's own, and most direct, messages are always in a code that is truly personal.

Larkin, like Housman, wrote a number of 'man-to-man' poems, most of which he never published, as Housman did not publish 'Some can gaze'. Some of them are outcries against being alone, or exclamations about thinking of girls in

bed with other men. The point is not that they are so different
from his immaculate and published poems, but that they have
confided themselves to a style of directness which does not
make use of the kind of secret and personal directness which
his poetry over the years found out, and worked on. Their
force is annulled, not by being the kind of complaint that
anyone might utter, but by being the kind of complaint that
many other people might have uttered in that way. Although
both Larkin and Housman depend on the clarity and
simplicity of the message, they depend much more on the
unique charge of personality in the code.

Soldiers are an important part of Housman's code.

> The street sounds to the soldiers' tread,
>   And out we troop to see:
> A single redcoat turns his head,
>   He turns and looks at me.
>
> My man, from sky to sky's so far,
>   We never crossed before;
> Such leagues apart the world's ends are,
>   We're like to meet no more;
>
> What thoughts at heart have you and I
>   We cannot stop to tell;
> But dead or living, drunk or dry,
>   Soldier, I wish you well.
>
>   (*ASL*, xxii)

As often in *A Shropshire Lad*, the blending of archaic and
colloquial speech is telegraphic. The redcoat whom we're like
to meet no more is historical and actual, as their second's
communication is both sober truth and fantasy. Everyone
recognizes the context. The meeting of eyes across the
crowded room: the woman or the man who might have been
loved. The eroticism of such a moment depends on the
acceptance of non-fulfilment; and the achievement, in words,
of fulfilment by other means.

The experience is as common as it is confidential. Hardy
confides it to us often in poems, but the special quality of the
experience here in Housman is the absence both of confidences
and of regrets. It has been freed from all the local and
contingent elements of longing or deprivation. It is pure
pleasure. The experience is as achieved as the poem with

which it is identified. As so often with Housman, decision and certainty bring total satisfaction, through the experience, to the poem.

> Such leagues apart the world's ends are,
>   We're like to meet no more;

and no regrets about that. The tone has the same reassurance and comfort as the ending of the sixtieth poem of *A Shropshire Lad*—'In all the endless road you tread | There's nothing but the night'—or the twelfth in *More Poems*—'Eternal fate so deep has cast | Its sure foundation of despair.' Nothing to worry about at all. The poem in its nature guarantees it. But the extra, and touching, reassurance here lies in its mutuality. Speaker and soldier seem not only to understand each other but to find their intimacy—total though of a second's duration—precisely in the knowledge that it is finished and complete, as the poem itself is.

If the soldier is also in some sense the reader, one of the young men whom Housman hoped would read his verse when they were in trouble, and he was not ('my chief object in publishing my verses was to give pleasure to a few young men here and there'), the reader is also privileged to be the soldier, in the moment while he is reading. The soldier is 'my man', a complex mode of address, going all the way from the patronizing ('When's the next train, my man?') to the comfortably possessive, as in German *mein Mann*—my husband. Housman's mode of address is of course unique to him, excluding patronage but not possessiveness: for at this moment he owns the soldier's being and thoughts, in the way that lovers own each other.

Indeed, the soldier's being changes progressively and subtly with the greeting to him in each stanza. The single redcoat who turns his head becomes 'my man' in the second verse, and plain 'soldier' in the last. At the end of *Antony and Cleopatra*, Charmian tells the guards who rush into the death chamber that the queen has done the right thing, as one descended of so many royal kings, to kill herself. That is in North's Plutarch, but Shakespeare adds 'Ah, soldier', as she feels the poison working on her, as if it were a last appeal for comfort. Housman too says goodbye on a note of appeal. It is a moment not unlike the one ironically imagined in 'From afar, from eve and morning' (*ASL*, xxxii):

> Now—for a breath I tarry
>   Nor yet disperse apart—
> Take my hand quick and tell me,
>   What have you in your heart.

A lifetime should be enough for any number of such exchanges, but the poem sees the whole of it as a moment, like that in which the redcoat turned his head. Here the idea of an urgency is heightened into mysteriousness, contradicted by the syntax of the interpolation—'for a breath I tarry | Nor yet disperse apart'—which suggests that the speaker has paused to get his breath back before asking the question on which the momentary meaning of life seems to hang. In the *De Rerum Natura* of Lucretius the spirit 'pereat dispersa per auras'—'perishes dispersed through the air'. With a hint in it of the soldierly 'Dismiss!', the English verb 'disperse' suggests an unavoidable military context, a request for orders, which in this poem never arrive.

> Speak now, and I will answer;
>   How shall I help you, say;
> Ere to the wind's twelve quarters
>   I take my endless way.

The poem as the message is vital to Housman: or the poem as a substitute for the message. In the redcoat poem, and in 'From afar, from eve and morning', the reader receives the message as if on behalf of the soldier, or on behalf of the friend whose hand the poet asks for. On receipt of the message the hand is not given; and the soldier on his way out of the poet's life can be granted nothing but a goodbye wish.

The humour that lurks here can become too explicit in another military context. 'Lancer' (*LP*, vi), chosen by Housman for *Last Poems*, and probably begun at the time of the Boer War, has more than a touch of camp baroque about it, too deliberately deadpan, although the tone is masterly in the way it celebrates military glory. There were successful cavalry actions in the war, which caught the public imagination, and the poem may also recall an episode from the earlier war in the Sudan, where the Lancers at Omdurman made a charge which cost a number of unnecessary casualties. The squadron ordered overseas 'A country to take and to keep' will be depleted when they are 'back from their taking and keeping'. And the unanswered question recurs as an ironic query: '*Oh who would not sleep with the brave?*' 'They ask and there is not an answer', and the question is referred by the dead trooper to his comrades who 'learned me the way to behave, | And showed me my business of dying'. It is also referred to the girls who will be 'eyeing my comrades and saying | *Oh who would not sleep with the brave?*'

Lines in 'Lancer' certainly make the hair stand up, but together with the preceding poem in *Last Poems*, 'Grenadier', it shows us a different Housman, a side of his personality which in its deliberately brutal simplicity can seem false. This is not communication but display. Excited and also deeply moved by the Boer War, in which his youngest brother was killed, Housman may have been jerked, as it were, out of his soldiers' and graves' imagination into a sense of the real thing, which required, in response, not his deepest, most telegraphic tones, but a show of his superbly athletic versatility. Kipling, whom he admired, and who was reported to him as saying, when both were old men, that he was right about poetry 'coming from the pit of the stomach', may have been in his mind. Kipling wrote a great burst of poems almost as part of his official affiliation with the war. Some are good, some bad. In 'Shillin' a Day' Kipling had drawn attention to a private's wage, which was also a retired soldier's sole pension, and this becomes the theme of 'Grenadier', and the last thought of a dying soldier for whom 'things will all be over then | Between the Queen and me':

> And I shall have to bate my price,
>   For in the grave, they say,
> Is neither knowledge nor device
>   Nor thirteen pence a day.

In spite of—perhaps even because of—the deadpan irony and the echo from Ecclesiastes, we seem outside Housman's own imagination here, the imagination that is very evident in another military poem, 'Soldier from the wars returning, | Spoiler of the taken town' (*LP*, viii). Housman told Sir

Sydney Cockerell that it was written 'Chiefly 1905', not long
after the end of the Boer War.

> Now no more of winters biting,
>   Filth in trench from fall to spring,
> Summers full of sweat and fighting
>   For the Kesar or the King.
>
> Rest you, charger, rust you, bridle;
>   Kings and kesars, keep your pay;
> Soldier, sit you down and idle
>   At the inn of night for aye.

Whether kaisers or caesars or kings, the soldier who has
earned his death can contemptuously dismiss them. To relax
at an inn, like his horse in the meadow, is the trooper's ideal.
Larkin's poem 'The Card-Players', as so often with that poet,
close in spirit to Housman's, imagines 'the secret, bestial
peace' of such a nocturnal inn. The grave as pub is an ideal
concept. In a letter to his sister the elderly Housman
remarked that his three pleasures were eating, drinking, and
sleeping. He was not, he said, a lofty-minded person.

As it happens, he is on record as saying that he liked
'Soldier from the wars returning'. He does not say why. But it
breathes a deep-concealed sense of fulfilment and satisfaction,
the physical relief associated with 'An Epitaph'. The soldier,
like the lover or the dead man, is 'whole of an ancient evil', has
achieved consummation and relief, as the poet who mentioned
that he had seldom managed to compose unless he was 'rather
out of health' achieved his own kind of wholeness and relief in
writing the poem. 'An Epitaph', whose title is not in the
manuscript and appears to be his brother's addition, suggests
that the ills of the ancient world are much like those of today;
even though Housman, in his Victorian infirmity, looked for
release from troubles which might not in ancient times have
seemed so heavy. But no doubt there would have been others.

> On Wenlock Edge the wood's in trouble;
>   His forest fleece the Wrekin heaves;
> The gale, it plies the saplings double,
>   And thick on Severn snow the leaves.
>   (*ASL*, xxxi)

The vigour here, so opposite to the calm of 'An Epitaph', makes a companionable point, none the less.

> Then, 'twas before my time, the Roman
> At yonder heaving hill would stare:
> The blood that warms an English yeoman,
> The thoughts that hurt him, they were there.

'Trouble' covers a lot of ground. A girl could be 'in trouble', and a man too, though it might be of a different kind. The Roman, like the wood itself, then and now, was no better off:

> The gale, it plies the saplings double,
> It blows so hard, 'twill soon be gone:
> To-day the Roman and his trouble
> Are ashes under Uricon.

'Better not to stay' was informal speech in the same way that 'Then, 'twas before my time' copies what the Shropshire Lad might be thinking, or what the weatherbound, tavern-frequenter is laying down the law about in 'The chestnut casts his flambeaux' (*LP*, ix). Housman is skilful not at imitating but suggesting relaxed or naive speech, and good at sounding judiciously commonplace. The two commas of 'Then, 'twas before my time' like a comfortable stretch after effort, make a stillness like history in the brisk riot of the poem's action. The Roman too is certainly there. 'Stare' takes on a Keatsian intensity as he seems to watch some prodigious sexual grappling, insistent in the repetitions of 'heaves' and 'heaving', of a sapling Daphne prostrated beneath the wind.

Like the wood threshed by the wind the poem opens and closes, its supple, live movement ending in the still and dead echo of the Roman name, all that is left in the last line. The poem bursts with a compressed power of language, and with Housman's implicit humour too, as well in image and movement as in acoustic tone. And yet the inner and invisible strife of sex, made visible in the heaving forest, does not seem put in deliberately. The images seem the very essence of spontaneity, unlike the artfully beautiful ones of the poem Housman composed, or at least completed, for *Last Poems* in 1922. 'Tell me not here, it needs not saying' (*LP*, xl) speaks of 'the pillared forest' which 'would murmur and be mine', and the traveller's joy that beguiles 'hearts that have lost their

own'. Those are fine phrases but they lack the tumultuous
play of Wenlock Edge, where no elegiac version of the Pathetic
Fallacy is sounded for the Roman and his trouble, nor for the
poet and his own.

The subtlety of 'On Wenlock Edge' consists in the way the
drama of sex and 'trouble' fills and agitates the poem,
embodied in the vanished Roman, the wind, and the trees.
The poet as Shropshire Lad can imagine the Roman of a
former time, but does not put forward his own feelings and
desires. But at moments he does just that, as if indifferent to
the extent he may be giving a sudden impulse or idea away.
Such an air of reckless confidences, sometimes conveyed in a
lengthened swinging line which heightens the impression of a
sudden impulse, is most effective in 'The lads in their
hundreds to Ludlow come in for the fair (*ASL*, xxiii). The
impulse in this superb poem is to convey the odd and
passionate message that it would be wonderful, among a
crowd of young men, to know which of them were going to die
young.

I wish one could know them, I wish there were tokens to tell
   The fortunate fellows that now you can never discern;
And then one could talk with them friendly and wish them farewell
   And watch them depart on the way that they will not return.

But now you may stare as you like and there's nothing to scan;
   And brushing your elbow unguessed-at and not to be told
They carry back bright to the coiner the mintage of man,
   The lads that will die in their glory and never be old.

'I wish' is poignant, and the whole poem wants to confide:
never mind if the confidence is thoughtless and unconsidered.
The bright line that seals, as it were, the certainty of the
poem's success also seems quite indifferent to the foolishness
of its own implication, for why should it be praiseworthy in
the coin to get itself out of circulation as quickly as possible?—
the coiner intended for it a long and useful time-span. But
very often in Housman such an apparent silliness conceals an
inner meaning. The lads brushing one's elbow who are born
to be hanged, to die young, to lie with a bullet in a distant
grave, are the ones who should be known—if only one could
know them—for a particular reason. They are the ones to

whom heart and services might be bound, and wishes confided—confided as the poet can only confide them now in his poem.

The next poem in *A Shropshire Lad*, 'Say, lad, have you things to do?', continues the same inner wish—to recognize, to join and work together, to be of service. 'Send me now, and I shall go; | Call me, I shall hear you call . . .' But in the Ludlow fair poem the wish for a secret means of identification is swallowed up in the sigh and the smile and the general friendliness thronging through the lines. The poem is made by the way its movement shrugs off what it also confides. Lonely persons, who like in general to be alone, also like fairs for their impersonal friendliness and contact in watching. Larkin twice describes fairs in very great detail, once in prose and once in verse; Housman has three poems about them. In 'The First of May' (*LP*, xxxiv) each man thinks 'The fair was held for him'. The poem's thoughts on time, change, and 'the sumless tale of sorrow', are concentrated on the very precise image of the state of orchards on the first of May:

> The plum broke forth in green,
> The pear stood high and snowed . . .

That is what matters, more than the commonplace of time and change; but 'The First of May' lacks in any case that inward confidingness which contrasts with the ebullience of 'The lads in their hundreds', and makes it such a memorable poem.

Housman never published another poem which has a similar kind of confidingness, one that seems deliberately to let itself loose in open bravado. 'I did not lose my heart (*MP*, xxxvii) is in its own peculiar way an admirable poem, which actually seems to depend for its effect on its power to embarrass the reader—no doubt the reason why the poet would never have considered publishing it—and on its uninhibited surrender to an emotional fantasy.

> I did not lose my heart in summer's even,
>   When roses to the moonrise burst apart:
> When plumes were under heel and lead was flying,
>   In blood and smoke and flame I lost my heart.

I lost it to a soldier and a foeman,
　A chap that did not kill me, but he tried;
And took the sabre straight and took it striking
　And laughed and kissed his hand to me and died.

Laurence Housman may well have rather approved the show-off element, and that may be why he included it in *More Poems* after friends advised him to leave it out. We can be glad that he did. However extravagant, it is a memorable piece, as much so as 'The lads in their hundreds', and in part for the same reason. The unexpected clue to the poem is surely in the contrast between the traditional world of love—summer, moonlight, and roses, which are boisterously and almost violently presented—and the world of war, which is yearning, languorous, and gentle. Comically insolent as it is, the transposition suggests the reader yield to it as the soldier who is speaking has done. It is the unlooked-for explosion of the verb—'burst apart'—which should be doing its work in the battle: but the battle itself is all graceful movement and languid surrender, the softness of plumes and heels, a gentle mime of swordplay, erotic abandonment, culminating in the laughing surrender to consummation. The poem has knowingly rejected the moonlit garden, as a place of conventional and mechanical loving, and chosen instead the bizarre softness and abandoned grace of a battlefield.

Often in his military dreams Housman seems to combine the rhapsodic note with that small internal voice of irony rarely absent in his poetry. In 'I did not lose my heart', he indulges himself in a variant of the once-popular scenario in which a proud, self-willed woman is swept off her feet by a masterly sheikh. He himself can be both parties, the loved one who is killed and the lover who kills him. In 'Lancer', a much more controlled and sardonic piece which Housman himself published in *Last Poems*, he can identify in a different spirit with the soldier who enlists and with the public who admires him. '*Oh who would not sleep with the brave?*' mingles Collins's 'How sleep the brave' with the sentiments of the girls who will be 'eyeing my comrades', and with the poet's dream of self as the soldier fallen in a far land, 'When back from their taking and keeping | The squadron is riding at home'. The light lilt in the rhymes and verbs—*lancer, answer; lying, dying; taking, keeping*—contrasts with the deep monosyllable of *home*; and the speaker himself has enlisted 'to ride on a horse to my grave', a line which manages to remain quite serious as well as disturbingly grotesque. It is also part of the poem's own kind of seriousness that it dismisses the politics of the matter with the insouciant news that the squadron has been ordered overseas 'a country to take and to keep'. By taking this action for granted the poem manages to draw attention to it, and more pointedly than any direct claim or comment in a poem of Kipling's could do. But although the poem draws attention to the soldier's function in an empire, it does not appear to do so deliberately. The poem is so engrossed in its own vision of the soldiers that it takes no more than brief notice of why they are sent where they are.

Housman's feelings for soldiers began early. On a trip to London in 1875 with his older cousin Mary he wrote home to his stepmother that they had seen the Guards on parade in St James's Park, and this was what had most impressed him. His stepmother, with whom he was on affectionate terms, had advised him not to miss the sculpture exhibition and the famous Towneley Venus. Francis Kilvert the diarist, whose Clyro curacy was a few miles across the Marches from Housman's childhood home, had viewed the tinted Venus with enthusiasm; but Housman preferred the figure of Mercury. His stepmother was not prescient; she showed good sense about a stepson just over the age of puberty. But the episode may suggest that it was not the meeting with Moses Jackson that made the first sexual appeal. Soldiers gave the opportunity for fantasy and wish-fulfilment which the friend did not. The single redcoat who turned his head belongs to the same class of inspiration as 'the chap that did not kill me, but he tried'.

At the time of the Boer War, in which his youngest brother was killed, Housman may have taken up again an earlier soldier piece. The notebook has a single verse:

> Kiss your girl and then forget her;
>   'Tis like the brave:
> They love the leaden bullet better
>   To sleep with in the grave.

The absence of what seems a needed alliteration in the first line calls for a more forceful word than 'kiss', a word which would accompany 'sleep' in the fourth. Housman was very likely aware of this, and Auden was no doubt equally aware of the suitability of another word, to be supplied by the reader if he wishes, when he makes the trooper in a Brecht adaptation cry 'Your breast, girl, quick, it's a crime; | The cavalry have no time . . .' (On the other hand, and on the matter of alliteration, Archie Burnett has pointed out to me that the true transcription of Notebook B. 204 starts '*Ay, kiss your girl and clean forget her . . .*')

'The Deserter' (*LP*, xiii) uses the same image for its ending ('. . . lie there with your leaden lover | For ever and a day'), but despite its use of conventional properties the poem has become, in Housman's curious fashion, a more personal one. As in 'Lancer', he identifies with both parties, in this case with the soldier and the girl, the forsaker and forsaken.

> 'What sound awakened me, I wonder,
>   For now 'tis dumb.'
> 'Wheels on the road most like, or thunder:
>   Lie down; 'twas not the drum.'

Housman's inner feelings give the situation an unusual intensity, which extends to an obviously cherished double meaning in a homely word:

> 'Hark, I heard the bugle crying,
>   And where am I?
> My friends are up and dressed and dying,
>   And I will dress and die.'

The military sense of dressing ranks goes with an echo of 'dressed to kill'; Housman's variation juxtaposes the everyday business of getting up with the soldier's equally everyday business of preparing to get killed. Nor does the poem let go of the ordinariness of getting up and ready:

> 'Reach me my belt and leave your prattle:
>   Your hour is gone;
> But my day is the day of battle,
>   And that comes dawning on.'

The belt brings out Housman's unique blend of parody with

inner intensity ('They braced their belts about them, | They crossed in ships the sea') but more important is the even-handed way the poem views the lovers, and the emphatic domesticity it rather surprisingly implies. This 'deserter' is leaving his home, and it is a desertion that matters to him, but he cannot help it: '. . . call it truth or call it treason, | Farewell the vows that were.' The poem knows what it means to women to have set up with men whose 'love is for their own undoing':

> 'Ay, false heart, forsake me lightly:
> 'Tis like the brave.
> They find no bed to joy in rightly
> Before they find the grave.

The awkwardness in the poem—'lightly' and 'rightly' is one of Housman's clumsiest rhymes—gives an unexpectedly earnest tone to the dialogue. Not for the first time, Housman seems to feel here what Larkin called the 'spearpoint' of a poem's emotion at the moment when he is working inside its convention. He knew what it was to feel deserted. His soldiers provide a refuge between the duty of loneliness and the longing for community. The single soldier who turns his head could also be looking for the girl he left behind him.

Philip Larkin, copying de Montherlant, liked to observe that 'happiness writes white'. A romantic poet (though he did not use the word) has a duty not to be happy. But for such a poet this can be happiness by other means, deprivation a way of getting in touch. His soldiers gave Housman a lot of happiness; and Larkin's conscious daydreams of pursed-up isolation did the same for him. Both poets are inspired by the far-off person—'bosomy English rose' or single redcoat—who can only find a being in a poem, and in meeting whom the poet becomes himself, his own personality. Larkin quotes a verse of Emily Dickinson:

> My life had stood—a Loaded Gun—
> In Corners—till a day
> The Owner passed—identified—
> And carried Me away—

and remarks 'this is romantic love in a nutshell, but who is its object?'* The object is the emotion that describes it, in a vision not unsuited to Housman's one of his soldiers. Capitals, dashes, and all—'Me' acquiring the status of a valuable but impersonal object—convey the absoluteness of expectation and identification. The owner, the other, is there, even if he or she or it never existed:

> It longs to smell the nitre
>   And play in sunshine warm
> And paint the soldier brighter
>   Than the Queen's uniform.

This odd image of Housman's never got past the notebook stage. It is the soldier's blood that longs to be released by the bullet to 'play in sunshine warm', the absolute moment that Housman dreamed of when he dreamed of his unknown soldier.

* Philip Larkin, *Required Writing: Miscellaneous Pieces 1955–1982* (London, 1982), 193.

CHAPTER 4

Personae

At the end of the last chapter I suggested that through Housman's mythology of soldiers, or Larkin's of deprivation, we become familiar with them in a way that would not occur if they told us directly about themselves or their troubles. We get what seems a private relation with them: one that is neither with a 'confessional' poet, nor with one who is creating himself for the benefit of his poetry and his readers. To carry Emily Dickinson's metaphor a little further, the loaded gun is waiting for the inspiration that will set it off. Towards the end of his lecture 'The Name and Nature of Poetry', Housman, who by then was sometimes putting on a conscious persona, remarked that he had 'two or three times in my life composed from the wish rather than the impulse, but I never succeeded to any purpose'. For most of the time, as he knew, he had been one of the poets who, as Paul Celan put it, expose themselves rather than impose themselves. A true poem by such a poet always finds him at home, and as if involuntarily so.

The counter-poet here is Yeats. He makes himself, style and poems, and they become true for us and for him in the act of creation. For the youthful Housman the discovery of self was so disturbing and disconcerting that poetry came as a way of disclosing it. Hardy's simple and wisely general view of the question was that the poet 'touches our hearts by revealing his own'. But there are different ways in which this can take place. When asked what it meant for him to be a poet Larkin said that it meant nothing, since he didn't feel that in the formal sense he was one. He had taken no steps to turn himself into a poet, and could not go to work with that label as if he were a doctor or a teacher. 'I don't want to go around pretending to be me.'

Housman might well have nodded his head sardonically. To be oneself is bad enough; to have to pretend to be oneself is ridiculous. But poetry can give intense expression to the concept of individuality. In *The Philosophy and Psychology of*

Personal Identity, Jonathan Glover considers claims for the existence of the self, and comes to the perhaps not very surprising conclusion that we are creating what we find to be ourselves all the time: the individual's sense of selfhood is continuously manufactured, like the cells of the body. Everybody knows this in some sense, but poetry feels and shows something more. It shows that the creature inside the poem is in some cases making himself; in others, discovering and revealing what only the poetry could tell him how, and in what form, existed.

The reader of this second kind of poet seems to get a sense of who the poet really is, which perhaps makes him wonder who he is himself. When a poet makes himself, the process is more dispassionately on view. The reader watches the poet at work on self-creation, and thinks: Could I do that too?—probably not. There is no envy but rather a sense of co-operation— helping the poet become himself. A philosopher might argue that the two processes are really one: all part of the complex extended process of self-creation. And yet it is in poetry that we can see a distinction between self-creation and self-recognition most clearly. The poet who discovers himself in his poetry becomes visible, as it were, through uncurtained windows.

Yeat's self-creation has an obvious element of showing off, even of parodying the process:

> Once out of nature I shall never take
> My bodily form from any natural thing,
> But such a form as Grecian goldsmiths make
> Of hammered gold and gold enamelling
> To keep a drowsy Emperor awake;
> Or set upon a golden bough to sing
> To lords and ladies of Byzantium
> Of what is past, or passing, or to come.

Such a rhetoric of make-believe would have seemed natural to any Renaissance poet, but Yeats gives it a specially personal dimension. His normal self is only, as he put it, 'the bundle of sensations that sits down to breakfast'; what he must become, and act out, is the poet as the creation of poetry. Auden, who understood Yeats from the inside, remarked with a twinkle

that in deciding to become a fabulous golden bird he was
telling 'what my nanny would have called "a story" '. But in
order to be himself and a poet Yeats needed a personal myth,
and extravagance was a calculated part of it. The self-made
bird might win the attention of the rich and the great, enthral
them with tales and gossip and prophecy. The journey to
Byzantium is not taken out of nature or after death; it is the
log of a poet preparing his own legend.

Egocentric, it can only use others in its myth. Yeats's
attempts to be human can be very jarring. 'Broken Dreams',
from the 1919 collection *The Wild Swans at Coole*, has a theme
that Hardy might have explored, or that Housman might in
his own way have touched upon. The poet has sat about all
day dreaming of his beloved—'vague memories, nothing but
memories'—and on the style of her looks—'From meagre
girlhood's putting on | Burdensome beauty'—to the present
time when she has grey in her hair.

> You are more beautiful than any one,
> And yet your body had a flaw:
> Your small hands were not beautiful,
> And I am afraid that you will run
> And paddle to the wrist
>
> In that mysterious, always brimming lake
> Where those that have obeyed the holy law
> Paddle and are perfect. Leave unchanged
> The hands that I have kissed,
> For old sake's sake.

The poet's wish to keep in his beloved this one natural
imperfection is intended to touch the reader; but Yeats's
creation of himself as lover surely fails to move his readers,
because it is so much preoccupied with its own image. The
physical shortcoming that should be homely and love-
enhancing becomes itself part of the legend that makes up the
poet. The lady has by implication obeyed the holy law by
completing the poet's fashioning of himself; even such an
endearing word as 'paddle' fails to domesticate the poem into
the fondness of true recall. Indeed the whole idea seems
slightly repulsive, in an involuntary sense, whereas the
calculated panache of the claim in 'sailing to Byzantium' is

truly magnificent. The accurate and tender, and thus moving, part of 'Broken Dreams' is in the reference to 'meagre girlhood', and the 'burdensome beauty' it must put on.

Housman's dreams are of a very different sort, revealing him as he is, not as a poet who becomes himself by means of them.

> I lay me down and slumber
>   And every morn revive.
> Whose is the night-long breathing
>   That keeps a man alive?
>
> When I was off to dreamland
>   And left my limbs forgot,
> Who stayed at home to mind them,
>   And breathed when I did not?
>
>   . . .
>
> —I waste my time in talking,
>   No heed at all takes he,
> My kind and foolish comrade
>   That breathes all night for me.
>   (*MP*, xiii)

What pretends to be a touching and involuntary memory does Yeats's poem no good. But Housman's really has something of the dazed air of dreams, and like dreams swarms with immanent meaning. Housman may have passed it over when he selected *Last Poems* because he felt it to be still incomplete. John Carter remarked on its apparently unfinished state, and Archie Burnett notes the presence in the manuscript, between stanzas two and three, of another verse fragment. The unfinished quality, so very unlike Yeats, suggests Housman's actual and personal absorption in an odd thought that has struck him. 'Whose is the night-long breathing . . . ? As Larkin puts it in his poem 'Ignorance', which has the same air of addressing a problem taken for granted all these years, 'Someone must know'.

And the someone who must know must be the one who unobtrusively performs this duty of living and breathing for the poet, a person simultaneously absent and present. The poem is filled not with personae—the poet and his beloved—but with their intense but invisible union in domesticity. The

breathing in bed of one spouse beside another is metamorphosed into a dream of changing roles. Each—poet and
beloved—become both the stay-at-home half of a relationship
and the half that roams abroad. The snug domestic concept of
'dreamland' (While I drift to dreamland | Safe inside my
slumberwear' writes Betjeman of a child going to bed after a
party) is where the poet goes, leaving his invisible comrade to
stay at home and mind, not the house, but his friend's 'limbs'.
'Off to dreamland', as it might be off to Africa or India,
suggests the negligence of the comrade who is footloose and
fancy free; but we know very well that the poet is the
homebound and housebound one: it is his friend who is far
away.

Poets like Housman or Larkin or Emily Dickinson, living
over the shop where their poetry gets written, are accustomed
to talk to themselves; while Yeats in his most intimate
moments is all the time addressing a hypothetical audience.
In Housman's poem the wasting of the poet's time in talking is
a comment—an ironical one—on the wondering seriousness
with which the two questions in the previous verses were put.
How strange it is for the poet to have what amounts to an
invisible partner beside him: a partner who is totally
indifferent to the fact, because unaware of it. But never mind
his unawareness. Simply by breathing he is a part of himself
for the poet, and so belongs to him. He is kind, because in his
physical being he cannot stop being for the poet what he is:
not only a life-saver but the source of the words the poem is
uttering. And it is clear that he is also foolish—here so
affectionate and spousal a word—because he does not and
cannot realize what all this means.

Meeting Housman or Larkin in their poems can be like
experiencing a change of consciousness. Poetry like theirs
gives us the abrupt feeling of what it is like to be someone else,
putting us in touch with them more immediately, and as
vividly, as might in other circumstances be the case with a
novelist and his characters. And the poet too has discovered a
different self in his poetry. Housman was a classical scholar,
Larkin a librarian, in the same sense in which Hardy was a
working architect and working novelist, and Emily Dickinson
a New England housewife. In a way, one kind of being

confirmed the other. Naturally they wanted recognition as poets, and yet in their poetry they did not become 'poets' but their own sort of person, 'whole', it may be, 'of an ancient evil'. Even the 'nobody' who Emily Dickinson slyly claimed to be, in the search her poetry makes for intimacy with a 'nobody' reader, was the special self into which her poetry made her.

This poetry becomes a self for the reader, and in his consciousness. At the end of his one talk on the subject Housman made his bow. 'I will not say with Coleridge that I recentre my immortal mind in the deep sabbath of meek self-content; but I shall go back with relief and thankfulness to my proper job.' That too is sly, as we should expect. Being oneself is not one's proper job. But its discovery in poetry can of course turn into a kind of formula. The inevitability of the process had no effect on Emily Dickinson; but it may in time have restrained, almost dried up, both Larkin and Housman. In their later poems they cannot avoid themselves, and sometimes give the impression of being a trifle acquiescent in the expertise of being. Then consciousness, both for us and for them, is confirmed rather than changed.

But the self it reveals is never altered. The poet like Yeats who makes himself as a poet also wishes to change himself as one: there is a clear distinction between a poet of the will, and a poet of personality. (Keats was one of the latter kind who strove, almost tragically, to be like the former.) Larkin's insistence that he had nowhere to 'develop' to a poet, and that such a development—as exemplified by Yeats—was for him a suspect process, is by implication true of Housman as well. The poem as self may be a discovery of what is wrong with self, but discovery can then contribute to its own kind of self-content. An unexpected thing about both poets, as I have stressed, is the feel of happiness the selfhood of their poems can give. (With the air of one hardly expecting to be believed, Housman's sister-in-law wrote that 'he always seemed to enjoy things and be happy'.) This of course is an aspect of the old 'sweetest song' and 'saddest thought' syndrome, the pearl of fulfilment produced by the grit of trouble in the oyster. And yet we know both poets precisely through the fixed being of that 'trouble'.

The change they can bring about in our consciousness—
'any time, any place', as Larkin put it—does not exist in the
case of a poetic stance which is developing or has been
developed; which may be, as it were, rolling itself towards
Eliot's 'overwhelming question', and 'the awful daring of a
moment's surrender'. For both Yeats and Eliot abasement is
part of the ceremonial of display. In *Little Gidding* the two
poets come together at dawn on the London pavement in a
formal pavane. They are expert at what Barbara Everett,
reviewing Lyndall Gordon's life of Eliot, has called 'self-
recrimination', the mixture of real uncertainty and true
diffidence with the sure awareness of how to present them
rhetorically. In 'Vacillation', Yeats performs a typically
ebullient variation on the theme:

> Things said or done long years ago,
> Or things I did not do or say
> But thought that I might say or do,
> Weigh me down, and not a day
> But something is recalled,
> My conscience or my vanity appalled.

Neither Housman nor Larkin could have produced that
virtuoso charade of vacillation, which does not ambush our
own awareness but is like hearing a man whom we do not
quite believe telling a story very well.

Our sense of critical admiration is very far from being the
response to what Owen Barfield, in his book *Poetic Diction*,
called 'a felt change of consciousness'.* Clearly Barfield had
in mind precisely the Housman effect: the physical sensation,
the suspension of judgement, the meeting in the words of a
poem with a new kind of self; and also the ensuing excitement
on the reader's part—although he may have read the poem
often before—an excitement that short-circuits him to the
emotion in the words, and to their author's unprotected being.
For Yeats, self-recrimination, or self-doubt, or vacillation, are
all part of the poetical manufacturing process. For Eliot they
form part of the willed spiritual journey behind the poem.
Both poets are, in a sense, reminding their readers of other

---

* *Poetic Diction* (London, 1934).

issues than the words of the poem, and thus nullifying the change of consciousness these might bring about.

To Housman, as also to Larkin or to Hardy, self-recrimination or incrimination mean nothing: their poetry does not work in those terms. Emily Dickinson knows nothing of it either. None of them have in their poetry the sense of guilt, sin, or uneasiness. This has worried some of their admirers. In his book *Poetry and Possibility*,* Michael Edwards writes of Hardy's poems on the death of his wife that 'it is troubling to reflect' how convenient her death was for the poet. It inspired him with a wonderful subject, and Hardy must have felt guilty about this, and have 'wished not to acknowledge the desire . . . to use his wife's death'. But do such considerations actually enter the world of those poems, and the change of consciousness they bring to the reader? Reading them like this shows a preference by the critic for a poetic climate of conscious and scrupulous reservation; as if the power to adjust and display his own awareness of the doubtfulness of what he is doing were itself an earnest of the poet's power.

So it may be, no doubt, in the later poetry of Eliot, or in the poetry of Geoffrey Hill today. Hill has made something of a speciality out of self-deprecation, and critics like Michael Edwards and Christopher Ricks admire him for this reason. Ricks is illuminating on the ways in which Hill's language picks its way among what he calls 'the tongue's atrocities'. The expression comes from Hill's poem 'History as Poetry', and is the title of Ricks's essay on the poet in *The Force of Poetry*.† Ricks feels it is the special grace of this sort of poetry to avoid such things, to avoid 'compacting or colluding the atrocities of which the tongue must speak, with the atrocities which—unless it is graced with unusually creative vigilance— it is all too likely to speak when it speaks of atrocities'.

A subtle point is being made here, and perhaps with an excess of subtlety, but we might feel that Hill's poetry is itself being invited to enter the area of critical attention to it. And this is a far cry from Housman, or from the poets I have been

* *Poetry and Possibility* (London, 1988), 128.
† *The Force of Poetry* (Oxford, 1984), 285.

speaking of in connection with him. Rather than bringing about a sudden change in the reader's consciousness, Hill's poetry may indeed appear designed to enter an academic mind, there to present itself forthwith for discussion and analysis. Ricks comments, truly enough, that 'the subject of much of Hill's criticism is the impulse of much of his poetry'. Certainly the poetry and the criticism are at one in the context of our attention, as if both were being proffered for academic debate.

Hill has praised Yeats's 'Easter 1916' as 'the tune of a mind distrustful yet envious, mistrusting the abstraction, mistrusting its own mistrust'. That is surely very perceptive. Yeats is defending himself in depth in his poem, and Hill in his poetry is doing something not very dissimilar. He explores the inability of his poetry to suggest what really happens in the world of action and suffering, except by an exact verbal exemplification of this inability. The process has its own kind of intensity, as well as its own kind of banality, for what Hill explores with such meticulous hesitations is what poems and readers have always taken instinctively in their stride. Poetry's tongue assumes and accepts the 'atrocity' in its utterance. So, for the matter of that, did Gibbon's tongue when it offered in a pair of perfect antitheses the cheering spectacle of a Mongol army filling a hundred sacks with the right ears of the slain.

Hill finds the subtle uncertainty of 'Easter 1916' deeply congenial. Yeats is seeking to assert that his poem should do what a poetry like Housman's unflinchingly does; and he makes the claim that 'a terrible beauty is born' without really believing it, but by compelling the poem to act out belief. The poem is full of a stylized misgiving, which the reader finds absorbing: he is admitted, not into the event, the fate and dreams of the rebels, but into the poet's self-consciousness in relation to them. Yeats parcels out his responses like a canny housewife, but when Housman writes of dreams he is the dreamer himself:

> My dreams are of a field afar
>   And blood and smoke and shot.
> There in their graves my comrades are,
>   In my grave I am not.

> I too was taught the trade of man
> And spelt my lesson plain;
> But they, when I forgot and ran,
> Remembered and remain.
>   (*MP*, xxxix)

Housman is not the least interested in what the reader may feel about this. The self-conscious element is notably absent. Housman does not want us to join him as poet and critic in the discussion circle. The lesson is his own (I owe to Archie Burnett the manuscript reading 'my' instead of 'the' in the second stanza, as in the present printed texts), and the reader is not invited to comment. At the same time, what the poet says is equally susceptible to enquiry, with the proviso that his words have not been coined in that spirit. They are genuinely estranged from the reader: whatever he may think is what the words of the poem do not. There is none of the collusion that critics of Hill, of Yeats, or of Eliot, are offered by those poets.

The 'felt change of consciousness' which Housman's words impose upon us is brought about by separation. He is not adopting the persona of a poet; his dreams are not made for us. Yeats, as he tells us in 'The Road at my Door', felt wistful about the visiting soldiers cracking jokes about war, 'As though to die by gunshot were | The finest play under the sun'. He turns away, 'caught | In the cold snows of a dream'. Yeats' dream of being a complete man, a man of action as well as dream, is one we are invited to share. Housman's is his alone. Something has happened to make him like that. He is not trying out in his poem the different personae of poet and soldier. In his prose poem 'A Letter from Armenia', Hill writes about 'the authentic dead', implying that anything a poet writes about them will necessarily be inauthentic. In a more sardonic spirit, Larkin writes in 'Poetry of Departures' about a home-lover's dreams of the authentic life, only to conclude, with a fine comic penetration, that no dreamed-of life can be anything but bogus. The poem's irony offers us the spectacle of the poet as unwilling stay-at-home and as dreamer who knows his dreams show him nothing except himself. But Housman's dreams of 'a field afar' are authentically thrilling because they changed his consciousness, and his poem about them changes that of the reader.

CHAPTER 5

The Romantic Personality

Now times are altered: if I care
  To buy a thing, I can;
The pence are here and here's the fair,
  But where's the lost young man?

—To think that two and two are four
  And neither five nor three
The heart of man has long been sore
  And long 'tis like to be.
                              (*LP*, xxxv)

The young man cleared off long ago, but also he is still here, more real than today's man. As Yeats says, 'Man is in love and loves what vanishes'. But the contemplation of what is distant or disappeared, or a country of the mind, is less important for romantic poets like Housman than the harsh actualities they contrast with. The important thing, as Larkin puts it in an unpublished poem, is to be 'able to view that clear'.

The star-filled seas are smooth to-night
  From France to England strown;
Black towers above the Portland light
  The felon-quarried stone.

On yonder island, not to rise,
  Never to stir forth free,
Far from his folk a dead lad lies
  That once was friends with me.
                              (*ASL*, lix)

The life sentence is also the poet's, and the friend dead for me is only alive in me. The feeling is transformed into a different setting in Larkin's poem, 'Maiden Name'. The name 'means what we feel now about you then'. It is that of a girl in the head, the home also of Housman's lads and soldiers, yet like that other girl in the photograph album 'in every sense empirically true'. The dead lad in Housman's mind is as graphically present in his vision of the isle of Portland as is the vanished girl in her photograph album.

By convention—and it is a convention whose many variations in romantic poetry are always potent and successful—such poems are all produced by 'a something' that has happened to the poet. Poetry takes over that arrest, turning it, as the oyster coats the grit with pearl, into compelling images of possibility, safe in the fact that they never took place. They become versions of an 'old story', the kind that Heine told in his poems. Housman learned from him how to be brisk and brutal about it, and so did Larkin at second remove. As he dryly observes about Emily Dickinson, 'writers are usually on surprisingly affable terms with their neuroses'. They can be on the same sort of terms with unhappiness, or love. In his review of R. P. Graves's biography of Housman, Larkin wrote:

To be more unhappy than unfortunate suggests some jamming of the emotions whereby they are forced to re-enact the same situation even though it no longer exists, but for Housman it did still exist. If unhappiness was the key to poetry, the key to unhappiness was Moses Jackson. It would be tempting to call this neurosis, but there is a shorter word.*

In ordinary life this might seem too common, too commonplace even, to be so compelling inside the poetry. Larkin implies that such things need a poem to be more than banal. The finality of the experience is drunk by poetry as if it were the best champagne. In his next sentence Larkin quoted Housman's view that 'anyone who thinks he has loved more than one person has simply never really loved at all'. This was perhaps a way of saying that unrequited love is the only real kind.

Housman's view is revealed in the poem he had written more than a quarter of a century earlier, after he had read of the suicide of a young Woolwich cadet. A copy of the letter the cadet had left for the coroner, in August 1895, was found among Housman's papers after his own death. 'There is only one thing in this world that would make me thoroughly happy; that one thing I have no earthly hope of obtaining.' The logic of the cadet's action must have appealed to

* *Required Writing*, 265.

Housman, who knew that obtaining what one longed for was not in fact the point. The cadet's letter is not only moving but expressed in a style Housman would have responded to: one of his own poems might have turned the colloquialism of 'no earthly hope' into literal fact, as the cadet's words had done. And his response was literal as well: a message to the cadet as brief, forceful, and intimate as the one to the soldier who turned his head. This is the poem beginning 'Shot? So quick, so clean an ending?' (*ASL*, xliv), beside which Housman put a newspaper cutting of the cadet's letter in his own copy of *A Shropshire Lad*. It is a poem I shall return to, a poem remarkable in its fervency and in the sense, so immediate in that first line, of effortless and instant communication. The poet who could confide in no one could do so with the cadet; and about something which had no chance of expression, except in a last letter, or in verse.

Housman's chances of being made thoroughly happy were also non-existent, and love, as he knew it, could not have existed if they had. But he manages to make his imaginative and erotic mythology even more compelling than his specific complaint. It might seem obvious to point out that the poems possess an eroticism in no way confined to his own source of unhappiness; but it is important to do so, for effect depends on the rapid alternation between a simple sexual self—the poet's own—and the longing and sadness of an intense, disembodied sympathy. Housman can transpose these griefs of sex ('Though the girl he loves the best | Rouses from another's side') without losing any of their erotic intensity:

> The weeping Pleiads wester,
>   And the moon is under seas;
> From bourn to bourn of midnight
>   Far sighs the rainy breeze:
>
> It sighs from a lost country
>   To a land I have not known;
> The weeping Pleiads wester,
>   And I lie down alone.
>   (*MP*, x)

The poem was written in 1893, using a famous fragment by Sappho. Three years earlier Jackson, now married, had

returned with his wife to India. We have no idea what
situation, if any, lay behind Sappho's poem. Both hers and his
are precise in the message, but not in its context, like the
anonymous verse of the sixteenth century:

> O western wind when wilt thou blow,
> The small rain down can rain?
> Christ, if my love were in my arms
> And I in my bed again!

C. S. Lewis opined that the reference was to the poet's wife,
not to his mistress: or he would have written 'in her bed
again'. Perhaps. Or a wife may herself be the poet. The point
is the emotion rather than the situation. In Housman's poem
the bourn is one of time and distance, the stroke of midnight
here and far away, the rain and wind blowing from the Welsh
Marches, the land of lost content, to just-as-distant India.
One land is irrecoverable, the other unattained.

The second version of this Sappho fragment makes the
grievance too explicit:

> The rainy Pleiads wester
> And seek beyond the sea
> The head that I shall dream of,
> And 'twill not dream of me.
> (*MP*, xi)

The notebooks contain what may be an earlier version of this,
in another metre:

> forgot,
> Lies in a land where I am not
> And lays to sleep beyond the sea
> The head that will not dream of me.

The first Pleiads poem is of experience all the more intense for
being unacted, even unimagined. It is 'the lost young man'
who is the erotic spokesman, rather than the poet all-too
aware that Jackson is not thinking of him.

In Keats's 'Hyperion' the fallen titans are compared to
forest trees, who 'dream all night without a stir',

> Save from one gradual solitary gust
> Which comes upon the silence and dies off,
> As if the ebbing air had but one wave.

The movement is as of the unsleeping who turn over and stretch out, 'from bourn to bourn of midnight'. The word is potent in English verse, and Keats wrote too that 'it vexes us to see beyond our bourn'. But the natural world is wide, although the lover lies rigid in his aloneness. There is an unexpected shiver of triumph in Housman's poems, when he identifies desire not with solitude but with the 'earth and skies' whose duration is in their own way just as finite.

> It shall not last for ever,
>   No more than earth and skies;
> But he that drinks in season
>   Shall live before he dies.
>
> (*MP*, xxii)

It is a function of the romantic personality—in poetry Heine's example was there—abruptly to 'drop all that nonsense'. 'Ho, everyone that thirsteth', unpublished in Housman's lifetime, is echoed in 'Spring Morning':

> Half the night he longed to die,
>   Now are sown on hill and plain
> Pleasures worth his while to try
>   Ere he longs to die again.
>
> Blue the sky from east to west
>   Arches, and the world is wide,
> Though the girl he loves the best
>   Rouses from another's side.
>
> (*LP*, xvi)

Love is no pleasure, but sex may be. Unexpected possibilities, proffered with a straight face, are an important dynamic in the poems. 'The scorned unlucky lad', like the 'lost young man', can see his affliction in a different light:

> Now the scorned unlucky lad
>   Rousing from his pillow gnawn
> Mans his heart and deep and glad
>   Drinks the valiant air of dawn.

The tone is like Larkin's trench humour. What the hell anyway? The heart, sad memorial urn of unrequited love, can also be briskly manned like a gun emplacement. And that possibility calls to another. Manning the heart for action, the

yet-untasted pleasures of living, can end in that other and
helpless moment of fulfilment, as in 'Eight O'Clock':

> He stood, and heard the steeple
>   Sprinkle the quarters on the morning town.
> One, two, three, four, to market-place and people
>   It tossed them down.
>
> Strapped, noosed, nighing his hour,
>   He stood and counted them and cursed his luck;
> And then the clock collected in the tower
>   Its strength, and struck.
>
>   (*LP*, xv)

The stanzas fill their seconds with the pauses of the clock,
their unhesitant deliberation a great contrast to the way in
which the verses about the scorned unlucky lad run rousingly
on into the challenge and enticement of morning. Housman
wished to drop that two-stanza poem on a hanging at the
proof-stage of *Last Poems*, but his brother persuaded him to
keep it. In 1928 Housman wrote to thank his publisher Grant
Richards for sending him a 'handbook' on the subject of
hanging, 'although the writer seems to be rather a buffoon'. It
can be a topic for buffoonery, as for gloating fascination, but
in spite of its details both of these are wholly absent from the
poem. It sets the image of a man who met his fate at an early
age, and was very conscious of having done so: a picture of
things gone irremediably wrong, of helplessness and ignominy
in extremest form. The clock in the steeple above the market-
place is a powerful symbol of mechanistic indifference to the
individual. The fate of the man to be hanged is that of the
romantic personality, in Housman as in Conrad, Nietzsche, or
Berlioz.

But the poem is not portentous about all this. It is as much
absorbed in its moment as the poems about the redcoat or the
cadet. Another poem in *A Shropshire Lad*, 'On moonlit heath',
takes the matter of hanging quite differently:

> They hang us now in Shrewsbury jail:
>   The whistles blow forlorn,
> And trains all night groan on the rail
>   To men that die at morn.

> There sleeps in Shrewsbury jail to-night,
>   Or wakes, as may betide,
> A better lad, if things went right,
>   Than most that sleep outside.
>   (*ASL*, ix)

The poet is now commentator: both casually well-informed ('They hang us now'), mordant, and sententious. The 'better man' sleeps his last sleep on earth, 'or wakes, as may betide'. The poet-speaker gives us a history of the business:

> A careless shepherd once would keep
>   The flocks by moonlight there,
> And high amongst the glimmering sheep
>   The dead man stood on air.

The footnote to the poem observes that hanging in chains was once called 'keeping sheep by moonlight'. As the poem progresses we realize that the commentator is, after all, closely involved. He is watching in the fields by night, where the flocks are grazing, and waiting for the morning, when his friend in Shrewsbury jail 'will hear the stroke of eight | And not the stroke of nine'. And yet the tone of the poem is not fully absorbed in its moment, as are the redcoat and the cadet and the man who heard the clock 'sprinkle the quarters on the morning town'. At their most effective the romantic personality, and the art that catches him in Housman's poems, are absorbed, and with complete apparent absence of self-consciousness. Here the tone is very conscious indeed; and it was a tone not lost upon Oscar Wilde, who would borrow it a few years later for 'The Ballad of Reading Gaol'.

In the last months of his life Wilde conveyed to Housman his admiration for *A Shropshire Lad*. He would have intuited its sexual background, but not have understood or found congenial the temperament and art that had produced the volume. 'The Ballad of Reading Gaol' has modernity in it in a vulgar sense: it speaks for the unfortunates, the misfits, those that have killed the thing they loved, the 'us' who have to swing or who rot in gaol. It is full of self-pity, generously but somewhat disingenuously unloaded on to all the rest of us. Housman is not a bit like that. Although 'On moonlit heath' is too conscious a poem, and not one of his best, it avoids striking an attitude, invoking compassion, marshalling the enlightened. On the contrary, the careless shepherd of historic pastoral and mythology becomes one with the lad that I know, to be hanged this morning in a shed behind the whistling trains. Only by the most tacit implication is he a victim of modern penology, as his predecessor of ancient barbarism. The insouciance of the word 'careless'—as a lady in *The Faerie Queene* can sing 'like careless bird in cage'—is stressed by the link in Housman's poem between fatalism and misfortune. The 'us' who are hanged in Shrewsbury jail are a long way from Oscar Wilde's 'us', the martyred band who suffer the horrors dealt out by an uncaring modern society. Housman was far from being in sympathy with the new ethos; and it is perhaps significant that on the one occasion he met E. M. Forster the two had nothing to say to each other.

Housman's romanticism does not go with the new enlightenment but with a classic acceptance of things. Christopher Ricks has indicated this in a passage of eloquent generalization:

Romanticism's pathos of self-attention, its grounded pity for itself, always risks self-pity and soft warmth; classicism's stoicism, its grounded grief at the human lot, always risks frostiness. What [is achieved] is an extraordinary complementarity; a classical pronouncement is protected against a carven coldness by the ghostly presence of an arching counterthrust, a romantic swell of feeling; and the romantic swell is protected against a melting self-solicitude by the bracing counterthrust of a classical impersonality.*

This might be taken to apply to Housman. It was in fact written about Philip Larkin. In tone and temperament the two poets undoubtedly correspond closely to each other; and not only his popularity and the classic-romantic structure of his work but its complex personality factor show Larkin's kinship with Housman. Their achievement comes more and more to seem not so much a balance of poetic styles as of the discovery of a means, in and through art, of being the way they are. Where Housman is concerned, Ricks's point was made more informally many years ago by H. W. Garrod, a classical scholar and also the editor of Keats, whose comments

* *The Force of Poetry*, 276.

on the *Thyestes* of Varius had once been roughly handled by Housman in the *Classical Quarterly*. None the less, Garrod's sense of the classics, as well as of English poetry, gave him a pretty good idea of how Housman's poetry worked, how it 'mans itself' to manifest in classic style a unique romantic personality.

CHAPTER 6

The Straitening

A poetry that 'mans itself' does so on a personal basis, without paying attention to a possible audience. Romantic personality is itself alone, with nothing communal or co-operative about it. This goes against the poetry, from Eliot and Auden to the present time, which often speaks as master or preacher, using the pronoun 'we'; and even when its tone is egocentric or confessional, as in the case of Lowell or Berryman, seeking to draw the reader compulsively into the poet's world. This poetry looks for intimacy while invoking solidarity. It has an air of responsibility on behalf of us all.

Auden disliked the public image involved, but could not avoid it. The image may also become an academic one, as so much poetry today is written on or near the campus. Poetry gets written to be read to a like-minded audience, and discussed by and with its members. Ricks himself writes of Larkin in the same spirit in which he writes in *The Force of Poetry* about Geoffrey Hill; and such an assumption of intellectual intimacy is not right for Larkin, although it is well suited to the tentativeness and the intelligence in Hill's poetry which courts that of his reader and critic.

Geoffrey Hill's phrase 'the tongue's atrocities' suggests embarrassments about the language of poetry which today are widely felt or accepted. Contemporary poetic diction is full of its own sensitivity, which seems part of its awareness of possible inadequacy. There are some things it cannot be expected to get its tongue around without sounding atrocious to itself, the 'atrocity' consisting in its own necessary enjoyment of what it describes. If those things were the Holocaust and the Nazi death camps, what then? Adorno said that language in art could not and should not try to take on such subjects, and the point has been made in various ways by other philosophers and commentators.

The poet can of course do it on a personal basis, as was shown by Sylvia Plath. Poems like 'Lady Lazarus' combined deep personal violence with the best horror properties: death camps and Nazi rituals, with God as Commandant. But the real violence was inside herself, feeding what she called the 'blood jet' of her poetry. With Paul Celan, from whose poem 'Engführung' I quoted at the beginning of Chapter 1, it is a very different matter. His poetry, published from after the Second World War up to his death in 1970, has been greatly admired, but its real nature seems to me to have been misunderstood, even by some of its admirers. Celan, who came from a Jewish, German-speaking community in Romania, lost both his parents in the Holocaust. Like Sylvia Plath he committed suicide, drowning himself in the Seine at Paris at the age of 49; but he was not, so to speak, a suicidal type, and his poetry did not depend like hers upon personal obsession and death-wish.

Although the events it referred to made Celan's poem 'Death Fugue' seem sensational when the volume of poems it appeared in was first published in 1952, it can now be seen to be a work of art which has absorbed those events so completely that they have become its own unique personality. Celan has done what other poets in the romantic tradition have done: made an absolute world, the pearl in the oyster, out of the inescapable material of his being. The great difference between his art and that of Sylvia Plath is that he had no will to do it; he does not use or compel the properties of an obsession. As he said himself, his poetry does not impose, but exposes, itself. The phenomenon is characteristic of a certain kind of art and poetry, and makes nonsense of the suggestion that a poet cannot 'attempt' to deal with certain kinds of subject-matter. No such attempt was made by Celan, as in another context it was not made by Housman. Adorno was misled about the nature of language in this kind of poetry, and in the nature of the creative source which produced it. Here the poet's tongue is not being 'atrocious' in saying what it does. It speaks with the innocence—in Celan's case the terrible innocence—of a totally realized individuality.

I believe it is revealing to read many of Celan's poems in the same way in which we read Housman's, not as a comparison but as an indication of the ways in which this kind of poetry does its work. And Housman's kinship with what might seem

quite other kinds of poetry is itself revealing. Celan represents
the same contrast of form to personality, of involuntariness to
technique. 'Death Fugue' is not a generalized or depersonalized outcry or lament, such as might be thought 'suitable' for
its subject, but a triumph of intense virtuosity, preserving a
deathly emotion in a poetic form which becomes and
expresses only itself. It adds, as R. P. Blackmur dryly put it of
such poetry, 'to the sum of available reality'. It does not
further extend an emotion or concept already known.

In an extraordinary sense, therefore, the reader of 'Death
Fugue', and of many other poems by Celan, enters a new
world when he reads this poetry, a new world which poetry
has created from the all-too familiar horrors of the old. No
wonder our contemporary ethos is made uneasy by this
romantic miracle, and can hardly bear to admit what has
happened, even speaking of the language of art in such a
context becoming an obscenity. Poets and critics today are
alike anxious to prove their understanding, compassion, and
commitment to whatever causes or questions may be around.
No one believes in the detachment of art from life, and indeed
such an idea is meaningless. We approve Wilfred Owen for his
pithy remark about his own verse: 'The poetry is in the pity.'
Owen was not deceived. But his poetry made a world of its
own in which the pity could live in terms of the art. No wonder
we are suspicious of the paradox. The feelings of the first
German readers of 'Death Fugue' must, one may feel, have
been a kind of relief—relief that the unhoused emotion had
found its way at least into art, created its new world. Not that
a terrible beauty was born. Yeats's give-away phrase is his
own poem describing itself: in creating its own world, 'Easter
1916' made its own admission. Following the immense success
of 'Death Fugue'—'Todesfuge'—with German audiences
Celan himself refused it to selections and popular anthologies.

The words of 'Death Fugue' make no admissions: only its
form does. Without pause or punctuation it repeats and
modulates in a fugue that is also a keening or dirge, making
itself from nightmare reports that have become clichés. The
blue-eyed master from Germany presides over guards who
force their victims to sing or play, and over coils and plaits of
hair heaped in a storehouse. These notorieties of the time are

eternalized in Celan's rhythmical lines with their compelled, hypnotic recurrences. German would be the only language for them; they would be at home in no other. But that is a truth familiar to poetry; and no other words in poetry would be familiar with these experiences, or with the poet who could utter them.

der Tod ist ein Meister aus Deutschland sein Auge ist blau
er trifft dich mit bleierner Kugel er trifft dich genau
ein Mann wohnt im Haus dein goldenes Haar Margarete
er hetzt seine Rüden auf uns er schenkt uns ein Grab in der
                        Luft
er spielt mit den Schlangen und träumet der Tod ist ein
               Meister aus Deutschland

dein goldenes Haar Margarete
dein aschenes Haar Sulamith*

As in much of his early poetry Celan uses a version of Hölderlin's classical metre, here blended and contrasted with the recurring phrases of the fugue. The space and sweep of the line, so majestic in Hölderlin and Rilke, retains a nightmare version of space as smoke, soot vapour vanishing.

Er ruft spielt süßer den Tod der Tod ist ein Meister
               aus Deutschland
er ruft streicht dunkler die Geigen dann steigt ihr als
               Rauch in die Luft
dann habt ihr ein Grab in den Wolken da liegt man
               nicht eng†

'da liegt man nicht eng'—'There one is not cramped'. The word is used of too-tight clothes, and here conveys a dreadful and paradoxical perspective of endless ease, lordly repose. There is the same appalling paradox in the recurrence of the hair—Margarete's golden, Shulamith's ashen—mixed

* Death is a master from Germany his eyes are blue | he strikes you with leaden bullets his aim is true | a man lives in the house your golden hair Margarete | he sicks his gang on to us he presents us a grave in the air | he plays with the serpents and dreams death is a master from Germany
your golden hair Margarete | your ashen hair Shulamith

† He calls more sweetly play death death is a master from Germany | he calls play the fiddles more darkly then you will rise as smoke in the air | then a grave in the clouds you will have there one is not cramped

terminally together. An assertive contrast between the hair of
a German and of a Jewish girl would not do; as it is, the
German girl makes a distracted appearance as totally separate
and unaware, but also as participant victim—Jewish girls too
had golden hair and German names.

A dozen or so years after 'Death Fugue' Celan wrote a poem
on the same theme called 'Engführung', a technical term for a
form of counterpoint in fugues. The word *eng* is again a key,
but this time instead of their terrible affinity with air and
heaven the poem's words seem to compress themselves into a
narrowing tunnel (the title could be rendered as 'Straitening',
'compression') in which there can be no turning back. This
gives its eerie tension to the lines I quoted in the first chapter:

> Verbracht ins
> Gelände
> mit der untrüglichen Spur:
>
> Gras, auseinandergeschrieben. Die Steine, weiß,
> mit den Schatten der Halme:
> Lies nicht mehr—schau!
> Schau nicht mehr—geh!*

It is startling to find that punctuation-marks and capitals at
the beginning of lines have returned, as if they were engraved
on stone. The appalling contrast here is between expectation
of the funerary place, sunk into propriety as memorial, and
the place, at once meaningless and meaningful, to which
consciousness, like the original victims, finds itself driven.
There is movement in the shadows of grass stems—haulms—
and in the multitude of grass blades, 'written-from-each-
other', like Housman's nettle that 'nods and curtseys and
recovers'; and the sense of inexpiable restlessness contributes
to the terror of the visitor, commanded to depart, while those
originally here were forced to stay. The passage and the place
are isolated, abandoned: in a context where the solidarity of
the dead with the living was once the first principle of
graveyard inscriptions. Those inscriptions, even the contemporary ones that are carefully simple and in good taste, claim
the communion of the living.

* Herded into the landscape with the unmistakable track: grassblades, written
away from each other. Stones, white, with the shadows of grassblades: Read no
more—look! Look no more—go!

But Celan's lines are not restrained, neither do they make any such appeal; even the command they utter is addressed to an absence, and seems given in silence. They seem not to try to communicate with us, still less to impress us. In the face of the poem's intensity the human convention of community with loss and suffering has quite vanished, and the first change in our consciousness may be towards relief, a relief we may find afterwards to come from our pleasure that art, in this context, has found a way to win. The cavils about aestheticizing the death-camps, the scruples that art here cannot try to say what we must feel, have been definitively set aside.

There is nothing of that sort to feel. This kind of poetry, as Housman would have well understood, arises from another source. Music is present, an echo of the orchestras that played in the death-camps, but all music is in a sense more silent, more separated from us, than are words. 'Engführung' constricts its fugal variations into 'nowhere . . . does anyone ask . . .' And the voiceless command not to read, to look: not to look, to go, echoes itself in a repetition of 'Night-and-Night', transforming into another dimension of feel the actual phrase used by the German exterminators—'Nacht und Nebel', 'night and fog'.

But after 'Night-and-Night', 'Zum | Aug geh, zum feuchten'—'go to the eye, to the moist one'. And later in the quite long poem, whose words seem at once effortlessly predestined and painfully laboured, there are other touchingly human appeals and gruesome reminders. But 'keine' | Rauchseele steigt und spielt mit'—'no smokesoul rises to join the play'—or is in the *Kugelfang*, the bullet-trap by the buried wall. Although there is a sudden burst of ghost song from the former choirs in the camp, hosannas that 'nothing, nothing, is lost', the terrible blankness is back in the end, with our senses 'herded into the unmistakable track', the grassblades 'written away from each other'.*

Obsessed by these deaths, and by the death of his mother

* In his excellent selection, *Poems of Paul Celan* (London, 1988), Michael Hamburger renders *auseinandergeschrieben* as 'written asunder', probably the only way to make it English, which 'written away from each other', hardly is. He renders *Kugelfang* as 'rifle-range', which is the usual English translation but fails to render in this context the special and claustrophobic meaning.

from the executioner's bullet in the neck, Celan wrote a tender
and much more accessible poem about her, 'Espenbaum',
('The Aspen Tree').

> Espenbaum, dein Laub blickt weiß ins Dunkel.
> Meiner Mutter Haar ward nimmer weiß.
>
> Löwenzahn, so grün ist die Ukraine.
> Meine blonde Mutter kam nicht heim.
>
> Regenwolke, säumst du an den Brunnen?
> Meine leise Mutter weint für alle.
>
> Runder Stern, du schlingst die goldne Schleife.
> Meiner Mutter Herz ward wund von Blei.
>
> Eichne Tür, wer hob dich aus den Angeln?
> Meine sanfte Mutter kann nicht kommen. *

The numbness of the poem is somehow combined with the
gentleness of tears. Driven into the bureaucratic slaughter-
house she was killed by the bullet, but the horror surfaces in
the poem as its opposite, in the mother's identity with the
poem. Our pity and horror are not pre-empted or invited. The
poem contrives an unpreconceived experience. Romanticism,
which is apt to be rather too assured of our general feelings,
'the human heart by which we live', possesses here the rare
implicit opposite of that propriety. We do not take the
sentiments of the heart with us to the poem, but rediscover
them when the poem has done its work.

At another point and period in the romantic spectrum,
Keats understood this, half unconsciously, and was uneasy
about it. In a well-known letter he writes of catching 'a
glimpse of a stoat or fieldmouse peeping out of the withered
grass—the creature hath a purpose and its eyes are bright
with it', and the human being has such a purpose too. 'But
then', Keats writes, feeling the need for a moral point, 'we
have all one human heart.' That is just what we do not have,
in the context of his own poetry, as of Celan's or of

---

* Aspen tree, your leaves glance white into darkness. | My mother's hair was never
white.
Dandelion, so green is the Ukraine. | My blonde mother came not home.
Rain-cloud, do you hover over the spring? | My quiet mother weeps for everyone.
Round star, you wind the golden loop. | My mother's heart was hurt with lead.
Oaken door, who lifted you off the hinges? | My gentle mother cannot come.

Housman's. Keats felt it necessary to authenticate his
perception as a poet by means of a properly universalized
sentiment. 'But then as Wordsworth says, "we have all one
human heart".' Not so for these purposes: it is the poem that
gives us its own one; and gives it to us individually.

Wordsworth's utterance assumes the universality and
sociability of response, but it is this sociability which is silently
denied at the opposite end of the romantic spectrum, nowhere
more so than in Keats's own poems. Keats's romanticism is
unique in its feel, the feel that is also unique in Celan's death
fugues and in the poem on his mother. The image of the
fugue—the word deriving from two Italian verbs, *fugere*: to
pursue, and *fugare*: to flee—express the paradox. The poem
compels itself into a uniquely narrow place, in which its being
is both an enduring and an escaping. The feel of both is
created within the poem, without reference to what is felt
about the subject outside it. The poem proposes a *new* mode
for feeling, necessarily separated from the general one.

Strangely enough, what is bestowed here on us by a certain
kind of art is also the premiss that Heidegger established in his
philosophy. For Heidegger poetry, the poetry of the Greeks
and of the German Hölderlin, was the true heroism of
language, the expression of what was most fundamental in
being. Celan felt a kind of tormented kinship with him, a
kinship tormented into obsession by Heidegger's former
connection with the Nazi party, and his silence—even after
the war—about the fate of the Jews. There was also a silence
between him and Celan, a silence the poet longed to break,
and which becomes eloquent in one of his later poems,
'Todtnauberg'. Todtnauberg was Heidegger's mountain re-
treat, and the poem commemorates a visit the poet paid there,
evidently in hope of talking about the thing which stood
silently about and between them, the Jewish tragedy.
Heidegger, whose philosophy was so grounded in the nature
of German poetry, seems to have been well versed in Celan's;
and Celan himself was deeply interested in the language of the
philosopher, inventing compounds in his poems like
heideggängerisch: 'moorwandering', a kind of pun on the name
as 'Moor-goer'.

And indeed the feel of the moor, the *Hochmoor*, haunts his

poem, which is also haunted by a kind of silence, perhaps that
of the philosopher himself. For, as the poet no doubt realized,
what could he have said? This poet himself was the only man
who could say it. His low-voiced, observing words in the
poem, about the place itself, convey a dreadful blankness in
nature about this 'beauty-spot' among the hills. In the
Hochmoor, on the *Waldwasen*, the woodland paths, 'orchis and
orchis, stand singly'. The reader remembers being driven into
that other and unmistakable landscape where the grass-blades
were 'written away from each other'. The 'half-trodden' tracks
on the *Hochmoor* are dumbly existent, yet full of a single
meaning: they are wet, very wet: 'Feuchtes, | viel'. The eye,
'the moist one', observes them. *Trocken* and *feucht*, dry and wet,
make frequent appearance in Celan. The dumb sense of the
wet moor, without human response in it, is silent and
expressionless, after the voices that cry in 'Engführung'.
There is no suggestion in the poem 'Todtnauberg' that
Heidegger's eye is dry; and yet the poem's impassivity settles
over a cry of protest, as inaudible as the owner of the
mountain chalet himself appears unseeable.

In a late lecture called *Zeit und Sein*, Heidegger begins by
remarking that a picture by Klee, a poem by Trakl, a theory of
Heisenberg, require an indefinite period of study before we
begin to see what they are about. The point suggests a further
point: that in all these cases we experience an immediate sense
of something quite outside our normal anticipation of things,
in words, or pictures, or propositions. In the case of the poem
it amounts to a sudden revelation of what the words of its
language are capable of being. And that being seems
indifferent to us, the readers. Celan's poetry carries this sense
of non-collusion as far as it can go, as in 'Engführung' there
are repetitions of the phrase 'Nowhere . . . does anyone ask
after you', and 'the eye, the moist one'.

The reader not only has the impression that he has never
seen such words before but that he is seeing them without any
of the fellow-feeling that comes from the speaker's wish for
collusion. Celan's cry to his own words, like the very different
example of Housman's cry, 'To this lost heart be kind', makes
no appeal to a third party. It is not communion the reader is
getting but the paradox of an involuntary intimacy. The

poet's unique speech deprives him of self-consciousness, which becomes corporate and communal. Celan was in every sense an intellectual, a teacher and translator whose own poetry became increasingly difficult to write and to read, but its language always produces that initial shock of the unique, of the felt change of consciousness, which in his own phrase made the poems like 'messages in a bottle'.

All this implies the deepest kind of division in the poet himself—in this kind of poet. The essentially romantic problem is stated in Hölderlin's epigram:

> If you have an intellect and a heart then only show one of them;
> Both will be condemned in you if you show them both at once.

Such a poet has created a world of words from which there is no going back, a return to being a man among men. Yet such a return is inevitable. The immediate and unique authority of what the poet has said told us something we did not and could not know: and yet in another sense, and as fellow human beings, we and the poet did know it. We knew about the death-camps and the scale of the war's horrors, and yet the absolute nature of Celan's poetry usurped that grimly relative and communal world of reported fact. It is clear that Celan was sensitive to this anomaly, and tormented by it, just as in his own way Keats had been. For none of these poets does Robert Lowell's modern orthodoxy of 'one life, one writing' make sense. Even the example of Hardy supplies its own droll confirmation of this, for the poet who daily 'noticed such things' was most inspired to poetry by the loss of his wife, whom when she was alive he had come hardly to notice at all.

The goddess Moneta makes the point on behalf of Keats in his second version of 'Hyperion':

> The poet and the dreamer are distinct,
> Diverse, sheer opposite, antipodes.
> The one pours out a balm upon the world,
> The other vexes it.

The point is always clear, though it may vary in application. Two people are concerned; and the poet, the Mozartian one, performs his involuntary office while the self-conscious 'dreamer' here meditates and agonizes over the sadness of

things. In the extreme case of Celan, the poetry even extends
its balm when the man who wrote it had his own horror
lodged in him like a fish-hook. Because of what had happened
to him, and to the world, he wrote what he could not take
back, and abandoned it, like the words in the bottle. Like
other modern poets he has been accused of 'hermeticism',
writing poems with meanings which only those in the councils
of his poetry could understand. This charge, which may have
played its part in the end in bringing about his suicide, he
rejected vigorously. His language and his poetry has its own
simplicity, as 'unmisgiving' as that of Keats himself. He could
not write poems that merely stimulate received emotions.
Keats was feeling towards the same knowledge when he said,
in a letter, that he wanted to write poems 'that cannot be
laughed at in any way'. Celan wrote poems that cannot be
cried at in any way.

   His suicide was in one sense an escape from what people
made of his poems and their alleged 'hermeticism'. Keats's
touching but naive idea was to make himself one person—as
with Lowell's 'one life, one writing'—by writing like a man of
the world, a knowing man among men. But the paradox
remained, for him and for poets like him. This inheritance of
romantic speech is unconcerned with the generalities of 'the
human heart', the touch of Wordsworth's 'truth in widest
commonalty spread'. Housman has his own way of being
unconcerned, as we shall see.

CHAPTER 7

The Name and Nature of Poetry

He exposes himself. The French word used by Celan, although the same in form, has other possibilities in English meaning. It has a technical sense concerning a sexual practice. Housman, who enjoyed and was something of a connoisseur of sex jokes, particularly, according to Maurice Bowra, those of a tasteless sort, would have been amused at the imputation. Equally, and at the same time, he might have been coldly angry. But a 'flasher' who exposes himself does so under some impulse as involuntary as that in the poet into whose mind verses arise as he takes his walk on Hampstead Heath. In May 1911 Housman wrote to the American poet Witter Bynner (who was to be a friend and correspondent of D. H. Lawrence) acknowledging his congratulations on becoming Professor of Latin at Cambridge, and replying to a query about his poetry. 'Of course it is nonsense when they talk about my "steadily refusing to write any more poetry": poetry does not even *steadily* refuse to be written by me; but there is not yet enough to make even a small book.'

'Not even steadily' was a good way of putting it. Housman was in some sense in a more fortunate position than Celan or Keats, who in their different ways show the same romantic paradox: the impossibility of writing poetry by the will and by preconception. Whatever the results, it has to be themselves— themselves exposed—and Celan's genius is the extraordinary and apparently impossible one of making what seems to be a predictable and external subject, the horrors of our age and the Holocaust, wholly unique and wholly himself. Keats and Housman only 'expose' themselves, if it can be put that way: but the element of 'wholly themselves' appears in the way they do it, or don't do it.

It would make no sense to speak of Wordsworth, or T. S. Eliot, ever being 'wholly themselves' in what they write. Their daily existence is in their pens: preconception and the will are as natural to their poetry as reflection and development and change of mind. Eliot's observations on personality in literature have a special significance here, for he was taking it for granted that personality in an author is a voluntary presentation, a matter of finding out how—in your writing— to be yourself. Eliot, for his own reasons, would wish to avoid doing that. But in any case the process does not apply to the poets I have been speaking of.

It would appear that much of the anguish of Celan, in the years before his suicide, was caused by other poets, critics, men of letters, the whole apparatus of literature, from which his own poetry is so remarkably separate. Keats suffered from the same exposure, which infiltrated the peculiarly vulnerable form of self-exposure constituting his poetic genius. Byron was not so very wide of the mark, after all, when he exclaimed with a mixture of derision and regret that Keats had let his soul be snuffed out by the articles of the reviewers. They had certainly made him want to write a kind of poetry alien to the kind he could write, removed from the poetic self he involuntarily was.

Housman's sensitivity was no less acute, but it was more adroit. His poems have an instinct both for revelation and for concealment, the two combining to create the kind of blankness and resonance that produced, for him, the physical sensations associated with poetry which he describes in his lecture. Its words make the hair stand up because they are working on us undercover. For Housman the idea of *hair*—its secret, independent response to poetic stimulus—seems to have been potent in a deadpan, even comical way. Did young Americans really write to him saying they would rather part with their hair than with their copies of *A Shropshire Lad*? The letter to Grant Richards in which he said so may have been one of his jokes; but the young and beautiful Absalom was hanged by his hair, and the Spartans before their last battle combed theirs on the sea-wet rock (*LP*, xxv): '. . . *He that stands will die for nought, and home there's no returning.*' Such a line moves within its own secret but perfect incongruity. Other young men are going bald over the years, jealously guarding the poems which keep them young at heart, whatever may have happened to their hair.

Yet parting with one's hair, in Housman's day, was decidedly a form of female sacrifice, as in Hardy's *The*

Woodlanders or O. Henry's story 'The Christmas Present', undertaken for selfless love or economic need. Comedy and sexuality, in any form, are never far apart, or far from pathos and the intimacy that goes with it. Near the beginning of 'The Name and Nature of Poetry', the lecture he was invited to give in Cambridge in May 1933, Housman quoted a stanza by the Elizabethan Samuel Daniel, from a poem about Ulysses and the Siren:

> Come, worthy Greek, Ulysses, come,
>   Possess these shores with me:
> The winds and seas are troublesome,
>   And here we may be free.
> Here may we sit and view their toil
>   That travail in the deep,
> And joy the day in mirth the while,
>   And spend the night in sleep.

Christopher Ricks, who has written so well on Housman, remarks on the apparent oddity of this choice of example, and suggests that 'the speaker is disowned or resisted even while we read and are attracted; the movement may be free and mirthful, but the whole sense of the lines is not so ... The emotional effect of Daniel's lines is not simple, and they did not come to Housman's mind just because of their fluent diction and movement.'

This must be true, and the matter may be connected more with Housman's sense of humour than with the fluency for which he praised Daniel's lines. What struck him about the stanza may have been a much greater incongruity than that between sense and movement. I remember being surprised and intrigued by this example of Housman's when I first read it, and sensing the presence of a submerged joke, part of the fairly elaborate tactic of kidding on the level which is practised by Housman throughout the lecture. The joke for him may have been partly in the recommendation to any 'promising young poetaster' of the modern age to lay up the stanza in his memory, 'not necessarily as a pattern to set before him, but as a touchstone to keep at his side'.

Matthew Arnold had recommended the use of such 'touchstones': shortcuts to aristocratic culture for a now widely educated society, samples of the very best poetry, ancient or modern, whose use was to teach the aspiring reader to know the best when he saw it. In a paper read in the 1890s to the Literary Society of University College, London, Housman gave his opinion that Arnold had been 'illuminating' in a way no other critic of his time had been. One source of illumination was no doubt these very touchstones, for Arnold's detachable examples of concentrated poetry came close to Housman's own view, expressed in the Cambridge lecture of 1933, that poetry could be not only detachable but nonsensical, and still be the purest poetry. On the other hand, a touchstone like the Daniel stanza, which the promising poetaster is advised to keep in mind, is not only as fluent and well disciplined as Housman's own verses but equally full of undercover meaning and suggestion.

After the Daniel sample he takes a verse from Logan's 'Ode to the Cuckoo', whose statement that the bird has a happier life than us carries 'a tinge of emotion'. Next, a quatrain from Dr Johnson's equally brief poem 'On the Death of Dr Robert Levet', in which homely sense is paramount, but where the same subdued emotion is in the stoic acceptance of a 'narrow round', in which there is more to be accomplished and endured than enjoyed. This leads on to the highest, a poetry for which 'there is no other name':

> . . . Duncan is in his grave;
> After life's fitful fever he sleeps well.

The two pregnant lines are packed with sense, both generalized and dramatically specific in Macbeth's case. Can Housman be deliberately selecting examples *particularly* pregnant with meaning, on the surface and beneath it? Such a suspicion is not dispelled by the other examples he gives of 'poetry neat', from Blake or from Shakespeare: 'Take O take those lips away', and 'Hear the Voice of the Bard'.

He does not deny that there may be a 'meaning' in Blake's verses, for Blake himself, or for his students who 'think that they have found it; but the meaning is a poor foolish disappointing thing in comparison with the verses themselves'. The point is valid enough if 'meaning' be taken to signify an interpretation, whether theological or hermeneutic;

but for his own reasons he says nothing about the power of suggestion, which is inescapable in such verse. He implies it negatively, however, in his most notorious example:

these simple six words of Milton—

> Nymphs and shepherds, dance no more—

what is it that can draw tears, as I know it can, to the eyes of more readers than one? What in the world is there to cry about? Why have the mere words the physical effect of pathos when the sense of the passage is blithe and gay? I can only say, because they are poetry, and find their way to something in man which is obscure and latent, something older than the present organisation of his nature, like the patches of fen which still linger here and there in the drained lands of Cambridgeshire.

The tone is urbane and witty, cool and detached, with nothing damp or swampy about it: in fact it is as 'blithe and gay' as the sense in the passage from 'Arcades' from which Housman is quoting, where the nymphs and shepherds are being invited to move to a more attractive and comfortable environment. None the less, that simile of the Cambridgeshire fen is revealing. Every class of gaiety floats in a pool of tears. Housman's blitheness is not a front, but a way of suggesting its opposite, and he has already anticipated those critics who have pointed out the fallacy in his argument: 'Housman's tears came from taking Milton's line out of its context and giving it a meaning it was never intended to have. By misreading Milton he has created what is essentially his own private poem.'* 'But of course', Housman might reply, well knowing that the area of privacy in a poem was precisely the area of exposure, the place where poet and reader met in their own way, and on their own terms. The fallacy exists, but is of a different kind, for Milton is not the kind of poet to meet Housman on his own ground; and in taking this example Housman is separating the poet wholly from his poetry, and concerning himself with his impression of the latter.

The examples from Blake and from Daniel are very different. There *is* a kind of intimacy in them, shared by 'the eyes of more readers than one': a revealing proviso thrown casually in by the lecturer. The Housman who held and

* F. W. Bateson *English Poetry: A Critical Introduction* (London, 1950), 15–16.

developed, probably insensibly, the views on poetry he came out with late in his life, is the same Housman who had given a paper on Swinburne to the University College Literary Society in 1910, the year after the poet died:

Mr Thomas Hardy has told me that in those days, when he was a young man of six-and-twenty living in London, there was a whole army of young men like himself, not mutually acquainted, who nevertheless, as they met in the streets, could recognise one another as spiritual brethren by a certain outward sign. This sign was an oblong projection at the breast-pocket of the coat. To the gross world of London, enslaved by commerce, respectability, and middle-age, it might have been anything; but the sons of fire who had similar oblongs protruding from their own breast-pockets knew what it was: it was Moxon's first edition of *Poems and Ballads*, worn where it should be worn, just over the heart.

Real poetry not only provokes physical symptoms, but symptoms that can be recognized in other people. Swinburne had been a real poet when he wrote of Aphrodite, but ceased to be one when he wrote of Liberty, for 'in truth poets never do write poems about Liberty, they only pretend to do so'. Liberty for Swinburne is a literary concept:

Books, he says, are to poets as much part of life as pictures are to painters. Just so: they are to poets that part of life which is not fitted to become the subject of their art. Painters do not paint pictures of pictures, and similarly poets had better not write poems on poems.

We know today, of course, that pictures may indeed be based on pictures, and poems on other poems; but Housman's point is none the less true of his own poetry, and of the kind that he thought of as real. It is the same point that he will make in 'The Name and Nature of Poetry'. Most people enjoy not poems but the poetical:

If a man is insensible to poetry, it does not follow that he gets no pleasure from poems. Poems very seldom consist of poetry and nothing else; and pleasure can be derived also from their other ingredients. I am convinced that most readers, when they think that they are admiring poetry, are deceived by inability to analyse their sensations, and that they are really admiring, not the poetry of the passage before them, but something else in it, which they like better than poetry.

The fallacy involved is of course obvious. 'The poetical' always merges with poetry, and there is no absolute distinction between the categories Housman is setting up. But what he detests, as he emphasized in the Swinburne essay, is poetry that is 'perpetually talking shop', whether Metaphysical, Augustan, or Romantic shop, or the kinds of Modernist shop of our own time. Poetry may be born from the poetical and depend upon it, as Housman himself depended on Heine or Eichendorff, Simonides or the Border Ballads, but only the poetical continues to luxuriate in its own medium. True poetry introduces its own new sort of reality.

This again is obvious; but the significant thing is that Housman takes for granted that real poetry can only be recognized by a few people, the young men whose pockets resembled Thomas Hardy's, or the young men who were prepared to lose their hair rather than their copies of *A Shropshire Lad*. The exposure involved is tacit and inexplicable; it does not depend upon literary skills or associations but on the personal factor, a setting 'up in the reader's sense a vibration corresponding to what was felt by the writer'. Again there is a hiatus here, for Housman seems not to confront the third obvious fact: that a physical capacity to respond to poetry, in his sense, is not necessarily contingent on a response to the 'vibration' it may set up. We do not have to be involved in a mutual exposure with the poet in order to have the experience described, as he says, by Eliphaz the Temanite: 'A spirit passed before my face: the hair of my flesh stood up.'

Would Housman have admitted this? I think so, but such an admission would have been part of his more general renunciation of the position he adopted in 'The Name and Nature of Poetry', and suggested much earlier in the piece on Swinburne. Of the latter he remarked, when urged to publish it: 'I do not think it bad. I think it not good enough for me', and the tone of that has the deliberate and stylized arrogance which he cultivated as a personal trade-mark. To a friend who asked for a copy of 'The Name and Nature of Poetry', he replied that he was not giving any. 'I take no pride in it. I would rather forget it and have my friends forget. I don't wish it to be associated with me.' The tone is chosen to avoid the pomposity of seeming indifference, but he is determined not to be caught defending an abstract position—and placed as one so defending it. To his brother Laurence he allowed himself, in a touching way, to be a little more laborious in explanation: 'I did not say that poetry was the better for having no meaning, only that it can best be detected so.' That was a real unbending. Laurence was also informed that 'a literary lawyer'* had written a book in which it was said that Hilaire Belloc was the best living poet, 'with the possible exception of you and me'. The letter was signed 'your still affectionate brother'.

Poetry can best be detected when its message is an intimate one, when the mode of exposure appears quite private. 'Appears', because such poetry seems to put its communication in the ear of the reader, in a language which only he could understand. In one of his last letters, to an American who wished to write a book about him, Housman cited the opinion given by another American—'I do not know where'—that his poems were the best since Keats. The perceptiveness of this unknown admirer, 'endeared to me by his amiable error', consists in seeing Keats's inimitable self-exposure as comparable to Housman's. Keats, who wanted to write poems 'that cannot be laughed at in any way', came to reject the unmisgiving self-exposure of his most characteristic poems. Housman did not have to reject because he never admitted. And his most sustained piece of 'criticism' is in fact an undercover work, teasing his audience by making them look in the wrong direction, and hiding the significance of sense and choice under the mask of the urbane scholar-poet.

Exposure in the context of poetry is for Housman always part of a secret joke, a joke which denies exposure by exploiting it. Only some would know, and if they did not, Housman could *feel* they did, just as he felt the presence of the young men reading his poems. ('The reputation which they brought me, though it gives me no lively pleasure, is something like a mattress interposed between me and the hard ground.') The word 'interpose' is both to amuse and to keep a distance. In going on to say that he 'cares very little about' his few lectures on other poets, or on poetry generally, Housman

---

* It seems to have been the author and barrister E. S. P. Haynes.

implies that he cares much more for the examples of poetry
that he gave in them. Each gives a clue, hidden in plain view,
to his true sense of and feeling for the subject. His gratification
that young men should like his verse was compounded with
his pleasure in talking to them under the rose, or talking to
any admirer in that urbane fashion. It is no doubt in this vein
that he tells us that 'even Shakespeare, who had so much to
say, would sometimes pour out his loveliest poetry in saying
nothing.

> Take O take those lips away
>   That so sweetly were forsworn . . .

That is nonsense, but it is ravishing poetry.'

Is it nonsense? Housman might as well say that 'When my
love swears that she is made of truth | I do believe her, though
I know she lies' means nothing either. Using the word
'nonsense' seems to be his way of saying that it means so much
to him it brings a shiver down the spine and a constriction to
the throat. Of course it does, as it would to any disappointed
lover who remains vainly and hopelessly attached to the
object of love. You cannot bring kisses again, which is why
you ask for them, and for the renewed relation they promise.

Housman goes on to say that the meaning of Blake's verses,
'My Spectre around me night and day', is 'a poor foolish
disappointing thing in comparison with the verses themselves'.
Again the disingenuousness is both obvious and opaque, and
it hides a point of real importance both for Blake's poetry and
for Housman's. For Blake, as Housman concedes, the verses
'probably possessed a meaning'; but they possessed quite
another for himself, which he prefers to say is no meaning at
all, but which he none the less displays before his audience
and his reader; hiding it in the open.

> My Spectre around me night and day
>   Like a wild beast guards my way.

Housman's Spectre was his own nature.

> A fathomless and boundless deep,
> There we wander, there we weep;
> On the hungry craving wind
> My Spectre follows thee behind.

> He scents thy footsteps in the snow
> Wheresoever thou dost go:
> Through the wintry hail and rain
> When wilt thou return again?
>
> .   .   .   .   .   .
>
> When wilt thou return and view
> My loves, and them to life renew?
> When wilt thou return and live?
> When wilt thou pity as I forgive?

How could he mistake the meaning that held for him? The unappeasable yearning is generalized in Blake's poem with as much simplicity as intensity. 'To this lost heart be kind'. Housman too could forgive as he asked for pity.

Yet it is certainly true, in another sense, that Blake's meanings can be disappointing, if not poor and foolish, as is shown by the verses that succeed the opening of 'Hear the Voice of the Bard', in which Blake makes his poem reiterate one of his mythic orthodoxies. The same might be said of the manuscript poem 'Never seek to tell thy love', in which a shrewd observation is made about the nature of men and women in the matter of love confidences. Love and affection proceed by silent accommodation, not by an insistence on 'telling all'. The loved one who flees from this too-abandoned confessional is met by one who woos her with such knowledgeable gentleness that she hardly knows what is happening.

> Silently, invisibly—
> O, was no deny.

Whether we prefer, as Lytton Strachey vehemently did, that revised manuscript ending, or the previous one, 'He took her with a sigh', hardly matters: both possess a knowing irony, the first having room for the previous lover's outburst of grief, the second for the breath of a second lover's consummation. But there is a discrepancy between the clarity of the observation—Blake's often sly and unexpected worldliness—and the gnomic mystery natural to his short poems, which Housman found to set up a 'strong tremor of unreasonable excitement in some region deeper than the mind'. Mystery and doctrine, mystery and good sense, are not always compatible in Blake's world,

and Housman sometimes preferred to suggest that such
incompatibility can have no meaning, even when it excites
him as poetry.

What did not excite him was poetry that used its form to
make 'a good point'. The 'intelligence' of the Augustan poet
meant that much of the poetry he wrote 'was excellent
literature, but excellent literature which is poetry is not
therefore excellent poetry'. Poetry may become noble by
expressing noble sentiments, but how much is nobility worth?
The uncompromisingness which poetic expression confers on
noble sentiment also entails a certain flatness. The gods of
poetry approve the tumult of the soul rather than its depth.

> Sorrow, that is not sorrow, but delight;
> And miserable love, that is not pain
> To hear of, for the glory that redounds
> Therefrom to human kind, and what we are.

What Wordsworth was saying must have caught Housman's
attentive eye. As a poet and reader of poetry he was a
connoisseur of miserable love that is not pain to hear of, or to
hold for ever inside oneself; and he knew all about sorrow that
is not sorrow but delight—at least delight for the reader. But
the way these things are expressed here, and Wordsworth's
characteristically blank use of the end-stopped line, set up no
tremor, and no vibration. About Emerson's uplifting
quatrain—

> Though love repine and reason chafe,
> There came a voice without reply,—
> ' 'Tis man's perdition to be safe,
> When for the truth he ought to die.'—

—Housman demurely observes that 'much' of the emotion
kindled by the verse can be referred to the nobility of the
sentiment', one on which a soldier might act without
concerning himself either with sentiment or nobility. 'Love',
we note, appears in both passages, but to be dealt with, both
by Wordsworth and Emerson, dispassionately and with
precision. Housman is equally precise about it, but his poetry
does not use it for purposes like these.

His climactic Blake quotation shows what Housman is

really getting at. It is one of the stanzas at the end of 'The
Gates of Paradise', headed 'To The Accuser who is The God
of This World'.

> Tho' thou art worship'd by the names divine
> Of Jesus and Jehovah, thou art still
> The Son of Morn in weary Night's decline,
> The lost traveller's dream under the hill.

This is 'pure and self-existent poetry, which leaves no room in
me for anything besides'. What Housman meant perhaps, but
did not say, was that the verse is packed with a sort of gleefully
genial intimacy of meaning, quite sure of its self, and sure that
those who understand will receive it. When Housman told his
brother he had not said 'poetry was the better for having no
meaning, only that it can best be detected so', he might have
added that we know it is poetry precisely because it has the
confidence to give us its own meaning in its own way. What
theological sense Blake purported Housman tells us he could
not imagine, and he felt no wish to learn; but he was well
aware that Blake was addressing his verses 'To The Accuser
who is The God of This World', the Satan of the Bible who set
up to be a judge of mankind, and who is thus confounded by
humans with the other judges whom they worship. Housman
liked verses to be touchstones in themselves, so he did not
quote the first of Blake's stanzas: possibly he might have felt,
in the lecture's context, some impropriety in doing so:

> Truly, My Satan, thou art but a Dunce,
> And dost not know the Garment from the Man.
> Every Harlot was a Virgin once,
> Nor can'st thou ever change Kate into Nan.

Blake here is enacting the part that a more enlightened and
poetic as well as more humorous Faust might have enacted
with Mephistopheles. His verse has the sinewy confidence of
its own conviction, but that conviction has nothing formal and
official about it, as with the examples that Housman took from
Wordsworth and Emerson. Blake seems to be outdoing the
mischievous spirit in mischief, his tone passing from affectionate disdain to rapt contemplation. Satan is prototype of
the rigid judge and moralist who cannot understand or

recognize the freedom of the human spirit; and humanity worships him as a god for this reason, for human beings always feel more comfortable when they have been issued with a commandment. But Satan is also in human eyes the son of the morning, a spirit of liberation and eternal dream of endless love, the love that Tannhäuser in the legend found with Venus under the hill. It is all part of the human comedy that we worship both repression, and the dream of freedom and happiness, lost or to come.

Blake's theology may not have interested Housman, but the vibration between his tones, his sense of things, his meanings in fact, clearly appealed very strongly. The Kate in him could indeed never be changed into Nan. The undercover paradox of his lecture is that it is really a study in the paradox of poetic *meaning*.

> Into my heart an air that kills
>   From yon far country blows:
> What are those blue remembered hills,
>   What spires, what farms are those?

The air that kills is also the air that gives life, the air of the land where poetry lives. It does not live, as Housman might have known very well, in a poem he published in *The Academy* in 1894 on the death, three weeks earlier, of Robert Louis Stevenson.

> R.L.S.
> Home is the sailor, home from sea:
>   Her far-borne canvas furled
> The ship pours shining on the quay
>   The plunder of the world.
>
> Home is the hunter from the hill:
>   Fast in the boundless snare
> All flesh lies taken at his will
>   And every fowl of air.
>
> 'Tis evening on the moorland free,
>   The starlit wave is still:
> Home is the sailor from the sea,
>   The hunter from the hill.

In his memoir, Housman's friend and colleague Gow noted

that this poem had been exhibited in manuscript in the Fitzwilliam Museum, but that Housman had destroyed the copy when he presented the museum with the manuscript of *Last Poems*. It gives interesting evidence of Housman's awareness of the vibration principle, its resonance sounding in unexpectedly different directions, and of the difficulty of making a conscious and studied use of it. Housman clearly came to dislike the manufactured feel of the poem, but its set element of vibration, centred at the sixth line, makes interesting use of the falsity in the poem complimented and commemorated—Stevenson's own 'Requiem'. The hunter and sailor with whom Stevenson identifies are revealed in Housman's poem in the pathos of their purely literary provenance. Stevenson's gifts can capture and exploit their prey; his imagination has its ruthless exorbitance ('the boundless snare'); and in being itself so wholly poetic Housman's poem accurately reveals the limitations of Stevenson's made-up world. 'The moorland free' is indeed the wide-open spaces as the writer annexes them.

In June 1902, after the Boer War, Housman published in *The Outlook* another three-stanza poem called 'The Olive', 'which', as he later wrote to Witter Bynner, 'is not particularly good'. It also seems to attempt explicitly to set up a hidden vibration, centred on the paradox of corruption: the corruption of the grave and that of war and finance, the sinews of war. On this basis the olive of peace should flourish.

> Close should the fruit be clustered
>   And light the leaf should wave,
> So deep the root is planted
>   In the corrupting grave.

Housman may have enjoyed fabricating these pieces at the time, but he knew them to be literature, in the sense in which he suggested and defined its properties in his Leslie Stephen lecture and opposed them to poetry.

The lines from Daniel he quoted there—'Come, worthy Greek, Ulysses, come'—were not absolute poetry, in the sense of meaning becoming one with emotion, lost in it until refound by the conscious mind, but they possessed that genuine vibration, 'corresponding to what was felt by the writer'; and they possessed as well that inner contradiction, between the 'set-up' and the meaning, which clearly fascinated Housman in the examples he took from Blake. Daniel must have been attracted, and quite poignantly so by the inner sound of it, to the cosy prospect of domesticity which his exotic siren is quite unexpectedly offering. The stanza's easy movement and comforting lilt may be at first incongruous with the notion of sirens, but the reader soon accepts it as entirely suited to this one. She offers a shared spousality ('Possess these shores with me') together with a snug leave of absence from the normal cares and responsibilities of wedlock, in work and child-bearing ('Here may we sit and view their toil | That travail in the deep'); while the concept of a good night's rest with a siren is all the more alluring for coming as such a surprise.

There is an odd affinity, which one may suspect that Housman relished, between the inner life of the Siren poem, and that of Blake's relation with his Satan who is God of this world. Satan and Blake are on as easy terms with each other as the Siren wishes to be with Ulysses; yet, metamorphosed into poetry, the relation acquires its own kind of mysterious-ness, *gives nothing away*. Where poetry was concerned we infer that Housman took special pleasure in such a relationship, and that the suggestion of it provoked the physical symptoms he associated with poetry.

For all that he depreciated the special order of 'shop' created by the Metaphysicals, Housman took pleasure in such unexpected conjunctions as these, conjunctions involving not a mutual and anticipated play of wit, but the sudden glimpse of a situation not normally revealed, or even imagined. The yearning of the siren was for the homely, peaceable, unsocial solitude of love, a felicity as unobtainable as that of the Owl and the Pussycat—or the ménage of Housman himself with Moses Jackson. That was indeed the lost traveller's dream under the hill. The 'meaning' of Daniel's lines for Housman lay in their invisible poignancy. We know that he took an equal pleasure in the nineteenth-century poet George Darley's poem about siren-mermaids. Though it belongs unmistakably to its period it might almost have been suggested by Daniel, for Darley was an accomplished pasticheur. 'George Darley was the writer of the excellent sham 17th century song "It is

not beauty I demand" which Palgrave printed as genuine in
the second part of the *Golden Treasury*.' 'Because it was so
good', Housman continues in a letter to his brother, 'I read
another thing of his, a sort of fairy drama whose name I forget,
and was disappointed with it and read no more.' The 'sort of
fairy drama' was *Nepenthe*, which had no success when
privately printed in the 1830s, at a time when such poems
were fashionable, but Housman singled out these lines about
the sea, 'a snatch of verse', as he told his audience at
University College Literary Society, 'whose author few of you
know and most of you never heard of':

> Hurry me, Nymphs, O, hurry me
> Far above the grovelling sea,
> Which, with blind weakness and bass roar
> Casting his white age on the shore,
> Wallows along that slimy floor;
> With his wide-spread webbèd hands
> Seeking to climb the level sands,
> But rejected still to rave
> Alive in his uncovered grave.

Housman was talking about Swinburne, and he comments
that although Swinburne was deeply attached to the sea he
had no idea how to describe it, whereas the man who wrote
this passage 'had seen the sea, and the man who reads it sees
the sea again'.

'. . . Not to transmit thought but to set up in the reader's
sense an emotion corresponding to what was felt by the
writer.' Larkin, as we have seen, put the matter in the same
way. The point is not an unexpected conceit, but a true feel of
the sea as Darley had felt it: its pathos, its helpless
aimlessness, forever 'floundering', as Hardy was to put it later
in *A Pair of Blue Eyes*, untidily among the obstacles along the
shore. This is the way Darley has really seen the sea—and
perhaps seen himself too?—and the way in which his poetry
manages to recall it, as Housman, in 'The winds out of the
west land blow' (*ASL*, xxxviii), hears on the wind the names of
friends:

> Their voices, dying as they fly,
> Loose on the wind are sown;

> The names of men blow soundless by,
>   My fellows' and my own.

The wind is as peculiar in Housman's poem as the sea in
Darley's, and carries in the same way poetry's instant power
of conviction, and equally instant lack of 'uplift'. The image of
names as visible as wind-blown paper is immediately
recognized. In 'Siren Chorus', Darley makes his sirens envy
the home life of the seals:

> Troop home to silent grots and caves,
>   Troop home, and mimic as you go
> The mournful winding of the waves,
>   Which to their dark abysses flow.
>
> At this sweet hour all things beside
>   In amorous pairs to covert creep;
> The swans that brush the evening tide
>   Homewards in snowy couples keep.
>
> In his green den the murmuring seal
>   Close by his sleek companion lies,
> While single we to bedward steal,
>   And close in fruitless sleep our eyes.
>
> In bowers of love men take their rest,
>   In loveless bowers we sigh alone;
> With bosom-friends are others blest,
>   But we have none—but we have none.

No wonder Housman responded to that. The poetical swans
who only brush the surface are equalled in delicacy by the
seals murmuring together like a human couple heard through
a bedroom door; but the seals are the real thing (as Aldous
Huxley observed, 'they make the poem'), the poem's balance
requiring, as Daniel's does, an equal mixture of the poetical
and the true inner vilnation, both the swans and the seals.
The climactic phrase or word is 'bosom-friends', which bursts
out like a sob at the end of the sirens' ritualized chorus. Its
spontaneity and unexpectedness is in marked contrast with
Housman's conscious attempt at a similarly climactic phrase
('boundless snare' and 'corrupting grave') in those two little
closest poems he repudiated, 'R.L.S.' and 'The Olive'.

Keats's use of 'bosom-friend' at the beginning of the 'Ode to
Autumn' achieves the same decisiveness that Darley's does at

the end of it, but with Keats it establishes acceptance and
contentment, and with Darley a touching chord of loneliness
and isolation. Darley's life was indeed sad and solitary; he was
very possibly a homosexual, like Beddoes, as Housman may
have intuited. More important is the *meaning* of such a poem
for Housman, the idea of meaning that is inversely explored
by his essay and by the examples in it, and which is connected
with the subtle processes of self-exposure and buried humour:
the two acting in partnership, and, as it were, exercising
protection and guarantee on each other's behalf.

Housman naturally had a nose for meaning, as a great
classical scholar and a brilliant emender of texts; but in a
more familiar manner he had a penetrating sense of how the
contract of meaning was set up in the mechanics of a poem, as
between the poet and his reader. The process often amused
him, or at least gave an occasion for his own kind of humour.
About specific poems and the construction of poems he gave
sharp, friendly advice to his brother Laurence:

What makes many of your poems more obscure than they need be is
that you do not put yourself in the reader's place and consider how,
and at what stage, that man of sorrows is to find out what it is all
about. You are behind the scenes and know all the data, but he
knows only what you tell him . . . how soon do you imagine your
victim will find out that you are talking about horses? Not until the
thirteenth of these long lines, unless he is such a prodigy of
intelligence and good will as I am: there you mention 'hoofs', and he
has to read the thirteen lines over again. 'Flank' in line six is not
enough: Swinburne's women have flanks. And as line six is at
present a foot too short I advise you to introduce hoofs into it; or
tails?

Laurence may well have been discomfited, but the advice was
sound, and his brother made up for the fraternal tease by
praising, no doubt sincerely, other poems in *Green Arras*, the
collection Laurence published in 1896, the year that saw the
appearance of *A Shropshire Lad*. Another letter to his brother
just before Christmas told how Housman had met a colleague
who supposed that Laurence was the author of both books,
('what a thing is fraternal affection, that it will stand these
tests') and added, in a PPS, 'I was just licking the envelope,
when I thought of the following venomed dart: I had far, far

rather that people should attribute my verses to you than yours to me.' The mention of venom removes its sting, and the tone is indeed affectionate, although Housman's real feelings were never on display, even to his brother, and his jests must have been hard to bear sometimes. 'The Great Ride', the poem about horses, is certainly one of the weakest in *Green Arras*; but the real interest of Housman's advice is the way in which it takes for granted, without saying so, that his brother's poem has not come off in terms of Housman's own test of poetry. The poet has failed to make an instant impression. '*How, and at what stage*' is the reader to find out what is going on? True poetry solves the problem by synchronizing the reader's sensation, his felt change of consciousness, with its meaning.

In construing poetical matter, as opposed to poetry in Housman's sense, the reader does indeed have to concentrate on what is going on; and many readers 'are really admiring, not the poetry of the passage before them, but something else in it, which they like better than poetry'. Readers of Wallace Stevens, say, are often in this state; and all readers—as we know but Housman does not say—would be well advised to experience it, and to add it on, as it were, to the primary sensation. D. H. Lawrence, as much of an 'élitist' as Housman, makes the same point about his own experience, comparing himself to a dog who pricks his ears and quests his nose at the feel of poetry, subsiding into canine indifference if the scent was a false one, but applying his human power of reason and appreciation if the poem is worth it. In a letter to *The Times* of 1928, Housman joined in a controversy about Shelley's meaning in his 'Ode to a Skylark', observing that although 'it is not one of Shelley's best poems, and enjoys more fame than it deserves, it is good enough to be worth interpreting'. He then cleared up the problem, which concerned the identity of the 'silver sphere':

> Whose intense lamp narrows
>   In the white dawn clear
> Until we hardly see—we feel that it is there.

One poet, T. S. Eliot, had pronounced that he had no idea what the thing was, or 'what the devil' Shelley meant;

another, T. Sturge Moore, had replied that 'a schoolgirl
would know that the "silver sphere" is the moon'. The textual
scholar put them right, pointing out that the object is the
Morning Star, the planet Venus, which disappears in the
dawn light as the skylark disappears in the brightness of the
noon sky. When the moon is a sphere at sunrise she is visible
in broad daylight, 'so that nothing could be less like the
vanishing of the skylark'.

There is an obvious comparison to be made with Housman's
incisive remarks on the meaning of his brother's poem.
Although the poet knows himself what he is talking about he
has failed to make matters clear to his reader. Felicitous and
accurate as is Shelley's comparison of Morning Star to
skylark's song, it has to be worked out; and Housman implies
that this is a reason for the poem not being one of Shelley's
best. The point is complex but revealing, because it shows
Housman's view of the matter in contrast to Eliot's, which at
the time was very much more influential and fashionable.
Eliot, like F. R. Leavis, assumed and censured Shelley's
romantic vagueness: Housman the textual critic realized the
precision of his poetic comparisons and metaphors, but
Housman the poet and theorist of poetry knew that this
precision did not make them poetry, in his sense. Shelley's
truest poetry was elsewhere, in the 'famous and beautiful lyric
entitled "A Lament", which . . . is known by heart to
hundreds of thousands'.

> Out of the day and night
> A joy has taken flight . . .

That is precise enough, but it is also poetry. It sends the shiver
down the spine, and that shiver may really be conditioned, as
Housman never quite admits, not by any mysterious agency of
'pure' poetry, but by the subject matter. 'Nymphs and
shepherds, dance no more.' Deprivation, loss, despair, become
a sad wisdom, an old humour. In the end, Housman cannot
bring himself to join up the two sides of himself; to say, what
he really knows perfectly well, that he values one source of
poetic emotion before all others—the lost heart, the lost life—
and that the 'Skylark' is not among Shelley's best poems
because its soaring precision is none the less rather facile and

blithe. It is not one of Shelley's 'sweetest songs' that 'tell of saddest thought'.

The development of thought, or of a personal philosophy in poetry, is one equally separable from the poetry itself. Wordsworthians are 'not noticeably sensitive to that thrilling utterance which pierces the heart and brings tears to the eyes of thousands who care nothing for his opinions and beliefs'. They are comforted—even Matthew Arnold was comforted— by Wordsworth's moral ideas, and by his 'conception of nature as a living and sentient and benignant being'; but 'these things, with which his poetry was in close and harmonious alliance, are distinct from poetry itself'. That is as close as Housman comes to admitting that it is not always easy to separate 'poetry' from poetical matter. He prefers examples from Blake, or from Shakespeare, where instant meaning—which he could perversely call 'nonsense'—came with the shiver down the spine. His soundest point remains that poetic meaning, in his paradoxical sense, does often appear different from the ordinary kind; and that if a poem is difficult or 'obscure', and yet successful, it has been able to short-circuit the normal lines of communication. It does so by instant collusion, very like the operation of a joke. Seeing a joke and feeling poetry produce immediate linguistic intimacy. Housman saw how close the two are in a poem like Blake's 'To The Accuser who is the God of This World', and for him 'the most poetical of all poets is Blake'.

By nature he preferred to isolate things, and in this lecture he was also trailing his coat, ignoring the obvious truth that poetic effect of all kinds is in the end joined together. Separating poetry from meaning was also to divide in himself the poet and lover from the scholar and textual critic. In a sense the two come together when he wrote poetry which reveals the man. But the process is involuntary, very different from the elaborate display of a 'self' which he deliberately put into the lecture of poetry, and which he none the less afterwards repudiated in his own fashion. ('I would rather forget it . . . I don't wish it to be associated with me.') There is a parallel between this self-display in the lecture and the display of himself in terms of style in some of his later poetry: 'Hell Gate', for example, in *Last Poems*. Both give the

Parnassian effect which G. M. Hopkins noted as characteristic
of the later Tennyson, and which could be defined as writing
deliberately like yourself. Tennyson ultimately wrote in a
Tennysonian fashion, and so did Housman in his own way. It
is a nemesis which is bound to attend on spontaneous
creation, the kind which, as Housman said in his own case,
'came into his head' rather than being 'composed'.

Housman was fully conscious of the problem, as it affects
what we must call romantic composition, and remarks on
Shelley's 'rule' of never changing what he had once written,
while Wordsworth 'tinkered endlessly', seeking to make his
composition a slow and organic growth. Yeats avoids
Parnassianism by altering and developing the style in order to
remake the self. A more reticent method, which appealed to
Housman, was to destabilize any tendency to write like
himself by deliberately exaggerating the process, until it
acquired a touch of the grotesque. Housman told a Cambridge
friend that he had been reading Edwin Arlington Robinson,
an American poet and seemingly imperturbable traditionalist,
who in the inter-war years, with Modernism in vogue,
continued to write lengthy poems in Tennysonian fashion on
Arthurian themes. Housman regarded most things American
with a more-or-less tolerant amusement, and we do not know
what he thought about Robinson's poetry. One of its great
assets, however, which he may well have caught his own
glimpse of, was the ability to deconventionalize normal poetic
language, at inconspicuous but surprising moments. In a
sonnet entitled 'The Sheaves', composed about the same time
as Housman's lecture on 'The Name and Nature of Poetry',
Robinson deploys a sonorously predictable octet about the
wheat-field ripening, 'And with a mighty meaning of a
kind | That tells the more the more it is not told'. That already
has a suggestion of deadpan parody on a romantic cadence;
and this is suddenly turned on in the startling image of the last
couplet, where the sheaves are husbanded (although the word
never occurs):

> As if a thousand girls with golden hair
> Might rise from where they slept and go away.

There is a touch of surrealism about that. We seem almost in the visual world of Matisse, or the metaphysical one of Wallace Stevens. It certainly fulfils Housman's requirement for the sudden recognition of poetry—'not to transmit thought but to set up in the reader's sense a vibration . . .' It escapes the predictability of the romantic Parnassian manner, just as do, in their different ways, the things that caught Housman's eye in Daniel's or in Darley's poems. They make an obvious contrast with the Parnassianism of late Swinburne, about whose 'Tale of Balen' Housman was elaborately sardonic in an excellent lecture addressed to the University College Literary Society in 1910, the year after Swinburne's death. Or with 'The Siren to Ulysses', a poem by the Victorian peer Warren de Tabley, who died a decade or so earlier, and who had in his day a discerning following among the poetry-reading class. De Tabley's Siren is in one sense as surprising as Daniel's or as Darley's, but not in the same felicitous way. She slips into the grave diction of a George Eliot heroine ('Wisdom is mine, but I can give thee love | Which, twinned with wisdom, is most perfect life'), and she caresses a responsibly bourgeois Ulysses with 'deep earnest eyes'.

Housman was to have his own methods for dealing with, or accommodating, the Parnassian tendency, and I shall consider these in a later chapter. In so far as it was an aesthetic aspect of nineteenth-century social convention, a reaction to it could be licensed in nonsense verses, like those of Lear and Carroll, and Housman indulged in the same form with skill and—when he was young—obvious high spirits. He brought to the art a particular demureness of concentration, which arrests the reader before he knows what its tendency is.

> Though some at my aversion smile,
> I cannot love the crocodile.

This animal, it appears, devours the naked children of Egypt in the interest of decorum.

> Then disappears into the Nile
> The infant, clad in crocodile,
> And meekly yields his youthful breath
> To darkness, decency, and death.

The poet affects surprise that society should be amused at his disliking a creature who performs such an acceptable social function. 'Purple William' is about a boy who tells lies and changes colour in consequence:

> The hideous hue that William is
> Was not originally his.

The matter-of-fact information has echoes of sin and lost happiness, of the discovery of the dreadful in oneself, of being sent to prison for the colour of one's hair.

The deadpan humour that Housman enjoyed putting into verse and often identified with the surprise of poetry, and its shiver of delight, was undoubtedly deployed in the composition of his famous lecture. It is in a sense humour Parnassianized, the quick process metamorphosed into a consciously and slowly unfolding affair which ends with a subtly ironic cartoon of the joker, the poet, himself: an elderly lad from Shropshire who has made more than good in the routines of academic life. 'Having drunk a pint of beer at luncheon—beer is a sedative to the brain, and my afternoons are the least intellectual portion of my life—I would go out for a walk of two or three hours'. It was thus that poetry arrived, from 'the pit of the stomach'. But not all hearers or readers of the lecture were beguiled by this account of the genesis of Housman's verse; or by the verse itself, and the theory of poetry its appearance suggested. In the next chapter I shall discuss the arguments of some of Housman's more or less adverse critics.

CHAPTER 8

A Voice in Opposition

Not without complacency Housman advised a friend that Eng. Lit. dons in Cambridge were complaining about his lecture. They said it had held up the cause of enlightenment, and of serious critical enquiry, by a generation. It must certainly have seemed like a voice from the distant past, for I. A. Richards had published his *Principles of Criticism* nine years before, and followed it with the significantly named *Science and Poetry* in 1926, and *Practical Criticism* in 1929. Literary criticism had become a serious study, almost indeed a science, and one especially receptive to the allusive and intellectual climate of Modernism. Good poetry required both training and intelligence to be properly appreciated by its audience. Stupidity about poetry, implied Richards, revealed a stupidity about life in general. A shiver down the spine got you nowhere.

Ironically enough, the new criticism and the new critics totally misunderstood the significance of Housman's touch-stone. That was natural, because he proposed it in what must have seemed then, and indeed still seems now, a deliberately perverse way. He was of course out to tease the new *bien pensants* of Cambridge, and the new critical arbiters. But the point about the shiver down the spine was that it happened to Housman himself, who described the way it happened; and Housman was a man who had been soaked in poetry and the classics all his life. In other words the primitive response, which he claimed by implication might be felt by someone with no experience of poetry and literature, was in fact a highly specialized reaction to a set of exceedingly complex stimuli, the unconscious product of voracious reading, feeling, and thinking. The student guinea-pigs whose reception of poems is recorded in *Practical Criticism* could not have been expected to have this reaction, or to base their judgements on it. Nor did they.

The conclusion Richards drew was that poetry needed to be

taught, and the difference between the good and the bad inculcated and learnt, as in any other form of study. Hence the revolution in English studies, which in thirty years raised status and morale to such heights. Where poetry was concerned, intelligence of response could be tested against the most obviously intelligent and complex type of poetry: Metaphysical, Augustan, Modernist. In that way the whole tricky question of instinctive pleasure and response could be bypassed: anyone capable of learning could learn what it was all about. Housman's touchstone, like that of Matthew Arnold (for Housman the only really 'illuminating' recent critic in the field) was based on an equally unspoken premiss: that only a minority of persons have the true feeling for poetry, a feeling that comes from a background of unconscious knowledge and appetite, emotion and experience. Some people funnel this into a receptivity for poetry: many people don't, and presumably can't, just as they may have no ear for music, and do not acquire one.

Arnold, the great educationalist in culture, saw no reason to admit openly that some people are more receptive to poetry than others. It is indeed a barren question, since so much depends on kinds of poetry, on fashion and generation and stimulus, experience and upbringing. For Arnold all poetry aspired to that of the Greek tragedians: for Housman, to a complex hybrid of classic and ballad, Blake and Shakespeare, romantic and German lyric. It was, significantly, just these types of poetry which the first readers of *A Shropshire Lad* would have studied or read for themselves at school. If they took instantly to what they read it was because their pre-conditioning in literature had prepared them for this new experience.

So much is obvious, and it may help to explain the reaction against Housman that came with the new principles of literary criticism, and the new university schools of English. Housman's poetry was still highly regarded, at least by I. A. Richards and William Empson; but 'The Name and Nature of Poetry' gave his natural opponents, at Cambridge and elsewhere, plenty of scope for reasoned objection. After his death in 1936 his reputation as a poet declined sharply in the pre-war cultural climate, although new poets like Auden

and Spender still admired him. This was partly at least for
emotional reasons; and indeed these early attacks on and
defences of the poet and his poems were made largely on
emotional grounds. It was not until 1945 that F. R. Leavis, in
the by-then prestigious magazine *Scrutiny*, devoted some close
criticism to Housman's actual poetic technique.

In what became Volume 13 of *Scrutiny*, for September of
that year, he drew a comparison between the first two stanzas
of 'Reveille', a poem from *A Shropshire Lad* (*ASL*, iv), and
Edward Thomas's poem 'Cock-Crow'. The piece came in a
series on 'Imagery and Movement in Poetry', the two eight-
line examples being set out in the way I. A. Richards had
done in *Practical Criticism*:

> Out of the wood of thoughts that grows by night
> To be cut down by the sharp axe of light,—
> Out of the night, two cocks together crow,
> Cleaving the darkness with a silver blow:
> And bright before my eyes twin trumpeters stand,
> Heralds of splendour, one at either hand,
> Each facing each as in a coat of arms:
> The milkers lace their boots up at the farms.

To make his two cases look the same Leavis took the liberty of
printing the first two stanzas of 'Reveille' as if they too made a
continuous sequence:

> Wake: the silver dusk returning
>   Up the beach of darkness brims,
> And the ship of sunrise burning
>   Strands upon the eastern rims.
> Wake: the vaulted shadow shatters,
>   Trampled to the floor it spanned,
> And the tent of night in tatters
>   Straws the sky-pavilioned land.

'Suppose one were asked to compare these in respect of
metaphor and imagery', wrote Leavis, there is 'a boldness of
poetic stylization that might be thought to constitute a
similarity'. But he goes on to say that such an appearance is
misleading:

. . . the metaphorical imagery is offered for its own sake, and (apart
from being beautiful and striking) not for anything it does: it

demands immediate approval, in its own right, as something self-sufficient and satisfying—we mustn't, for instance, ask what becomes of the burning ship as the silver flood mounts (or does it?) and full daylight comes. The function of the imagery here, in short, is to hold the attention from dwelling in a realizing way on . . . the actuality ostensibly invoked.

Leavis may well be right to suggest that the opening of the *Rubáiyát of Omar Khayyám*, with its vigorous metaphors for daybreak, could here be an unconscious source of inspiration. But Housman's imagery is both 'simple and simple-minded', with the poet seeming merely to say: ' "Here is poetical gold: take it! Here is radiant beauty: be moved!" ' Leavis concludes that 'the kind of beauty offered values itself implicitly at a rate that a mature mind can't endorse'.

The 'mature mind' and 'adult' attitude to experience required by Leavis are capable, none the less, of stock response, and this seems an instance of it. I. A. Richards valued the 'ironic' above all as a touchstone for poetry, and Leavis seems unaware that both poems are, in their different ways and styles, examples of what Richards had in mind. He is indeed fully conscious of it where 'Cock-Crow' is concerned. The poet there 'has humoured himself in a half-waking dream-fantasy which, when it has indulged itself to an unsustainable extreme of definiteness, suddenly has to yield to the recognition of reality'. The reader may indeed be gratified to find himself taking the same attitude to the experience that the poet is taking: that of a rueful, amused understanding of fancy and fact, and their interrelation—an attitude Leavis found satisfying to a mature mind. The reader feels no change of consciousness, but shares in the poet's wry amusement at what poetry fashions out of the experience, a process Leavis suggests very well. It is the chief effect of Edward Thomas's poem that it claims very little for itself: the absence of claim underwrites its success. Even the diction succeeds by a kind of modesty: 'heralds of splendour' is substituted in the manuscript for 'of equal glory', and both phrases seem in their context acceptable, rather than the second thought being wholly 'right'.

Edward Thomas wrote many much better poems, as Leavis would no doubt have agreed: more moving poems, and ones more characteristic of his own insight and psychology. But the crucial point for Leavis—his own touchstone almost—is the attitude which the poet is taking to his poem. To take such an attitude, and to show the reader that you are taking it, is for Leavis virtually the definition of the desired poetic 'irony'. Leavis perceives and analyses—a pioneering practice at that time—just what was Thomas's attitude. Was he indulging 'the pleasures of stylisation?' It might seem so, but he isn't. Instead he is pondering the implications of his attitude with a 'subtlety of organisation' directly comparable to the lack of it in the Housman example. Thomas's attitude is 'subtly conveyed and subtly developed'.

'Cock-Crow' was probably influenced by Robert Frost's poetry, and by what Thomas in a letter to Frost affectionately referred to as 'North of Bostonism'. One of the poems in *North of Boston*, the collection which was so much to inspire Thomas, is 'The Wood-Pile', a poem intimately related to 'Cock-Crow' both in the felicity of its effect, and in the attitude the poet takes towards that effect. Both imply rather insistently the kind of wisdom, or maturity, approved by Leavis; and imply it most of all in the studied casualness which Thomas (whose poems end up being very different from Frost's) somehow avoids. The poet in the wintry swamp finds an abandoned wood-pile and wonders who made it and why it has been left

> far from a useful fireplace
> To warm the frozen swamp as best it could
> With the slow smokeless burning of decay.

Meticulous in its relaxation (the wood-pile is 'older sure than this year's cutting, | Or even last year's or the year's before') it 'scores'—as he himself put it—just as it was intended to. The relation between the reality of things, and what we can fancy about them, is similar to that in 'Cock-Crow'. True, the fancies of poetry sharpen our sense of reality, which is the point of the business, but we still wryly recognize them as fancies: that, indeed, is a crucial aspect of what Leavis recognizes as 'maturity'.

So there can be no spontaneity of emotion, no direct feeling? Frost measures his wood-pile ('four by four by eight') as Wordsworth once measured his little pond in 'The Thorn'

('I've measured it from side to side | 'Tis three feet long and
two feet wide'), but 'The Thorn' is excited and absorbed in its
own pathos, and the wood-pile is measured in order to set
homely reality against fancy. Its first readers laughed at the
pond in 'The Thorn': the tone in which Frost's facts are given
is very different. The poet is his subject's master, not excited
and absorbed by it; he is writing a poetry that winningly
shows, as part of the poem's effect, how and why it is getting
the effects it does.

This kind of tone is here itself a touchstone for Leavis, and
going on to apply it to Housman's poem reveals for him the
latter's weakness. 'Whereas Housman's poem depends on our
being taken up in a kind of lyrical intoxication that shall speed
us on in exalted thoughtlessness, satisfied, as we pass, with the
surface gleam of ostensible value, Edward Thomas's invites
pondering (we register that in the movement) and grows in
significance as we ponder it.' The pondering Leavis envisages
is in tune with the way the poem itself goes, but it is surprising
that so acute a critic should not have felt able to consider
'Reveille' in the same way. He was put off by the dash of it, the
air of a virtuoso performance, and the 'exalted thoughtlessness' suited to it, and this distaste stopped him seeing that
after the first excitement and the felt change of consciousness
there could be a good deal to be pondered in Housman's lines.
The crucial difference between them and Thomas's is that the
process of appreciation of the latter is continuous, and
continuously involved in an intimacy with the poet's own
attitude. Housman's give us the first shock of pleasure and
surprise, followed by the different wish to know what lies
behind it. Leavis, as one would expect, preferred his reception
and the poet's attitude to be, as it were, academically whole.
But Housman's poetry, and the poetry he referred to and
defined in his lecture, does not work like that. The contrast it
offers between a first impact and the time of consideration
(which may or may not follow) is always marked: and for
some readers the first may seem to make the second
superfluous. The urgency is the point, the 'Up, lad, up,' with
which 'Reveille' goes on after the opening stanzas; the thrill in
'Take my hand quick and tell me . . . Speak now and I will
answer'. But even a masterpiece like 'From far, from eve and

morning' (*ASL*, xxxii), probably made no great appeal to
Leavis.

In his Swinburne essay Housman praises the poet Darley's
description of the sea, from *Nepenthe*, because 'the man who
wrote it had seen the sea, and the man who reads it sees the
sea again'. Its very extravagance bursts into fact; and the
same is true of his own verses on daybreak. Anyone who has
ever watched a spectacular sunrise sees it again in the poem.
Cloud-flakes take on shapes in the rising light more fantastically than at sunset, as the light from the east defines them
more sharply. Housman was the first poet in English to use
'dusk' in the sense of dawn; a usage memorably repeated in
'Little Gidding', where Eliot, on the suggestion of a friend who
offered the phrase, has his poet meet an apparition in the
'waning dusk' of a wartime morning. 'The silver dusk' of
'Reveille' is echoed by the night and sleep that await us in the
last stanza, enhancing the urgency of dawn to a young man
avid for all the world offers. The flamboyant images of sunrise
startle the reader, half sardonically, into a sense of the
extravagant excitement of being alive . . . being dead cannot
compare with it.

It is surprising Leavis should not have noticed the virtuoso
comedy in those two first stanzas. Housman's tone can be
baffling, it is true; and never more so than when he uses, as he
does here, the emphatic trochaic measure he referred to as 'the
Laura Matilda stanza'. In *Rejected Addresses*, the lively collection of parodies of contemporary poets published in 1812 by
the brothers James and Horace Smith (it includes a particularly amusing and discerning one on the tactic of Wordsworth
in the *Lyrical Ballads*) there is an artless Della Cruscan poem
by 'Laura Matilda'. The stanza form, wrote Housman to his
colleague J. W. Mackail, 'I think the most beautiful and most
difficult in English', and three years later he was congratulating
Bridges on his use of 'the old and beautiful stanza, now
unjustly despised because so often ill-managed . . . which
ought not to be left to Laura Matilda'.

Leavis makes no mention of Laura Matilda, nor of the
stanza form and its rewards and difficulties. Possibly he
thought poetry in that style a hopeless case. But Housman's
view is revealing, because he composed several poems in this

form, including 'On the idle hill of summer' (*ASL*, xxv) and
LP viii, 'Soldier from the wars returning' (*LP*, viii). ' "Lydians,
lords of Hermus river" ' (*AP*, i) has the same metre; and so—
the most interesting case, to which I shall return—has 'The
Land of Biscay, (*MP*, lvi). Housman told Mackail that he was
'too fond of it', and his brother noted that because of this 'he
always doubted the merit of any poem in which he had
succumbed to its attraction'. Certainly he never included the
Lydian or the Biscay poems in any collection. But the
dangerously haunting charm of the metre made a strong
appeal; and, more than that, offered a challenge to his power
of escaping from its naive 'beauties', and the guileless
earnestness of 'Laura Matilda'. In taking up the challenge
Housman must have wondered in some cases whether the risk
had some off.

But not, presumably, in the case of 'Reveille' in *A Shropshire
Lad*. There the change of consciousness the stanzas produce is
as spontaneous as it appears to be unexamined. Housman's
attitude is well hidden: hidden behind an emotion without an
attitude towards it. The comic, the incongruous, and the
grotesque are there, but the poem does not comment on them;
emotion sweeps them along, and the reader too, until he can
reflect on them later. The incongruity of all the fireworks in
the dawn of 'Reveille' brings out what Larkin calls, in his
poem 'Sad Steps', 'the strength and pain of being young',
indivisible from their own kinds of lyrical absurdity. Not
wanly climbing the sky like Shelley's, the moon in Larkin's
poem glares through his bedroom window at 4 a.m., flooding
him with the blankness of memory. The surprise of the moon,
like the shock of Housman's sunrise, brings even in vulnerability its own image of the grotesque ('There's something
laughable about this.') As with Darley's sea, or Robinson's
girl-sheaves, the picturesque is turned into a powerful
congener of immediate sensation.

To be sure, Larkin's poem is 'taking an attitude' much
more overtly than Housman's, but it also confronts us with
the same surge of emotion and response. 'Attitude', in
Leavis's sense, is explosively alive, and yet undercover, in
Housman's phrasing. Leavis objects that the function of his
imagery 'is to hold the attention from dwelling . . . on the

actuality ostensibly invoked'. But he seems to miss the
comedy of signs in Housman's language, here expressed in the
contrast between the forceful elegance of his fantastic metaphor and the hearty simplicity it arouses, and identifies with.
Something in the poem longs to be as simple as its 'actuality':
that of young men fast asleep in the dawn, and their
incoherent greed, on waking, for all that experience can
afford. That avidity for all the world offers is both touching
and comic, and is met by a wonderful mixture of precision and
banality in the poem's fourth verse.

> Towns and countries woo together,
> Forelands beacon, belfries call;
> Never lad that trod on leather
> Lived to feast his heart with all.

Landscape is personified into explicit amorousness; forelands
are like foreheads gleaming with curls. In the same spirit the
coming of dawn ('the silver dusk returning | Up the beach of
darkness brims') is in the stealthy form of dusk—boats
creeping ashore on the last tide of darkness to surprise the
sleepers—and the metaphor bursts into a conflagration both
spectacular and comic, as if the craft were stranded and on
fire: 'rims' suggesting a mechanical predicament. The expressive word 'straws' ('Straws the sky-pavilioned land') has
the depth of a yawn and a sprawl, and suggests the
composition of the mattress in the fifth verse:

> Up, lad: thews that lie and cumber
> Sunlit pallets never thrive.

The vigorously comic syllables return us to the comedy of
dawn which burst upon the poem's opening, pulling open and
dismantling a dark tent to reveal the pink pavilion of sky.

The play of reference and image in the poem gives it an
inward drama; it swarms with indications and contrasts of
longing and regret which its own headlong *tenue* seems to
ignore. The shiver of response to 'Hear the drums of morning
play' may seem all the poem aims at, as if the message to wake
and get up were coincident with its physical impact and the
felt change of consciousness. The final exhortation:

> Up, lad: when the journey's over
> There'll be time enough to sleep.

is predictable but also surprising, after the overwhelming
briskness of morning. Solitary oddity—that of the maker of
metaphors for the fantasy of sunrise—not only contrasts itself
with the call to action ('. . . blood's a rover; | Breath's a ware
that will not keep') but mixes the helter-skelter of action into
the metaphors themselves. These seem designed as if to
appeal to the young persons exhorted to get up and grab what
they can of life's good things: and this strategy of appeal is
part of their comedy. It was a successful strategy. Very many
young men, not otherwise perhaps very susceptible to the
pleasures of poetry, were to take this fantastically and yet
fastidiously emphatic language in their stride, and to their
hearts.

   That remarkable popularity, extending up to his own time
and place, may itself have something to do with Leavis's
adverse criticism. Academics prefer a kind of poetry to which
they themselves can act as mentor and advocate. But the more
vital point is Leavis's rational and communal attitude: what
he called the technique of saying to his fellow-reader: 'This is
so, is it not?' A poem stood or fell on the intelligent discussion
of it; and like I. A. Richards, he took for granted a distinction
between a 'simple and simple-minded' poem and its readers,
and the response of what he called 'the mature mind', one that
had been educated and conditioned by the close study of
literary texts. The operation on the reader of *A Shropshire Lad*
abolishes any such distinction, but Leavis could scarcely be
further from the case than when he states that Housman is
only peremptorily offering us 'poetical gold'. 'Reveille' is
indeed both peremptory and emphatic in what it offers, but
not by drawing attention to itself. Its urgency seems a way of
getting to and at the sleeping young, whether they are
poetically inclined or not. Even though there is much it in it
for a reader to find, it makes no distinction between its
readers. Its message is precise and clear: what is complex is
the way it is conveyed, and the personality behind it, and
these are not matters to which it invites attention. If we pay
such attention we are, as it were, on our own. What is
certainly not in the poem is the note of collaboration which
Leavis identifies with 'maturity', and which he finds—correctly
on his premisses—in Edward Thomas's poem 'Cock-Crow'.

Of course Housman poems can be susceptible to reasoned criticism of the kind Leavis made. From his point of view a better example to have taken would have been such a poem as 'On the idle hill of summer' (*ASL*, xxxv):

> On the idle hill of summer,
>   Sleepy with the flow of streams,
> Far I hear the steady drummer
>   Drumming like a noise in dreams.
>
> Far and near and low and louder
>   On the roads of earth go by,
> Dear to friends and food for powder,
>   Soldiers marching, all to die.
>
> East and west on fields forgotten
>   Bleach the bones of comrades slain,
> Lovely lads and dead and rotten;
>   None that go return again.
>
> Far the calling bugles hollo,
>   High the screaming fife replies,
> Gay the files of scarlet follow:
>   Woman bore me, I will rise.

Famous and memorable as it is, this poem seems to be hollow inside, and less satisfying than 'Reveille'. Not now sounding the call, but himself the passive object of its appeal, the poet cannot make the same brilliant use of the exaggerative mode. Its use here becomes a cliché ('None that go return again') which does seem to affront the reader's sense of what is right. Nor does it help to see the thing in generalized symbolic terms: the soldiers as men born of women, facing until they are dead the hard slog and dangers of existence. The middle stanzas lapse into indulgent overstatement; 'lovely lads' relies too much on a Shakespearean echo, and is not bracing and effective as are the clichés of 'Reveille'. As William Empson observed, many Housman poems—he instanced 'Tell me not here, it needs not saying' (*LP*, xl)—present what he thought a silly idea in compensatory terms of extraordinary beauty and deftness. But other and complex factors are at work in such cases, which cannot be found in 'On the idle hill of summer'. It lends itself not to its own parodic subtleties, and its own kind of humour, but to the kind of external parody which both

addicts and detractors of Housman have amused themselves
with. The concocted 'misprint'—'women bore me'—was
already an old joke when Empson reported that his Japanese
students, finding Housman's attitudes quite familiar, wrote
essays mentioning that if women bore you you should join up,
and that it is better and more honourable to be dead.

Housman's use of his exaggerative mode can seem wonder-
fully spontaneous. The man who says 'Wake' in 'Reveille',
and says it with such a flourish of comment on the baroque
spectacle of dawn, is very different from the dreamer who
hears the drum, and seems already to have prepared his stock
response and the terms in which to express it. Yet it is clear
that Housman uses a satirically emphatic manner to mislead
about his own feelings by expressing them with such stylized
force. That sense of a pose would also have irritated Leavis,
but it makes its own effective use of conventional ballad and
lyric topoi, giving them a private emphasis that never disturbs
the convention. They leave intact the solitude of the poet's
own experiences but make them appear to be common to all
('Then, 'twas before my time, the Roman . . .'), and that is the
way the poet seems to like it.

There is a surprising diversity of these common topoi within
the boundaries of *A Shropshire Lad*, and the readiness to use the
most commonplace of them must also have irritated the new
critics. The two poems that follow 'Reveille' ironically fulfil
its promise of feasting the heart. The speakers in 'Oh see how
thick the goldcup-flowers' (*ASL*, v) are the young man
walking among the flowers with his girl, and the girl herself:

> . . . Then keep your heart for men like me
>   And safe from trustless chaps.
> My love is true and all for you.
>   'Perhaps, young man, perhaps.'
>
> Oh, look in my eyes then, can you doubt?
>   —Why, 'tis a mile from town.
> How green the grass is all about!
>   We might as well sit down.
> —Ah, life, what is it but a flower?
>   Why must true lovers sigh?
> Be kind, have pity, my own, my pretty,—
>   'Good-bye, young man, good-bye.'

In the last verse-and-a-half of the poem there is a quiet growth of the unexpected, among the conventions of the form. In the stumble of the metre, cunningly conveyed in the first line of the last verse, there is audible not only the excitement of the young man but his unsureness, an oddly realistic lack of confidence. In the next poem, 'When the lad for longing sighs' (*ASL*, vi), the girl is warned that she can take the young man's trouble on herself:

> Then you can lie down forlorn;
> But the lover will be well.

So ends the hopeful morning awakening, when 'blood's a rover'; and the barely noticeable pattern in the three-poem sequence—many *Shropshire Lad* poems seem arranged in groups of three or four—provide a small dramatic sequence; again of the kind that would find no favour with criticism in the 1920s. But what is personal in them merges with what is conventional in unexpected ways. Housman himself had found the extent to which love is 'speechless', the key word in 'The True Lover' (*ASL*, liii):

> Under the stars the air was light
> But dark below the boughs,
> The still air of the speechless night,
> When lovers crown their vows.

It is Housman's version of the ballad motif: the dead lover coming to his mistress. The dialogue follows its time-honoured course, with the girl wondering why her lips and neck are wet.

> 'Oh like enough 'tis blood, my dear,
> For when the knife has slit
> The throat across from ear to ear
> 'Twill bleed because of it.'

Perhaps it was the recollection of such things which pre-determined Leavis's impatience with the opening of 'Reveille'? Hardy once expressed annoyance at reviewers who supposed some of his verses to be unintentionally comic, rather than deliberately humorous, and Housman may have felt the same, although one doubts that his early readers were inclined to smile. That reaction came later, in a more sophisticated age.

It is true that neither poet has a light hand with this type of humour. Their true humour is elsewhere: in Hardy's feel for things and places; in the understatement beneath Housman's neat emphases, in this poem the speechlessness behind the lovers' exchange. Through the dead lover's display of grim wit is revealed the poignancy of speechlessness and the quality of darkness, noticed as Hardy might have noticed it:

> Light was the air beneath the sky
> But dark under the shade.

Though the lovers may be stylized they are not derisory. The clue in 'Oh see how thick the goldcup flowers' is the alternation between the young man's crafty platitude—'Ah, life, what is it but a flower?'—and the stumble in 'Look in my eyes then, can you doubt?' That look goes with the speechlessness of Donne's lovers 'who watch not one another out of fear', and has its own sad version in 'Look not in my eyes' (*ASL*, xv):

> One the long nights through must lie
> Spent in star-defeated sighs,
> But why should you as well as I
> Perish? gaze not in my eyes.

Love unreciprocated finds its own kind of silence. The Narcissus of 'Look not in my eyes' is as ruthless in his own way as the lover of 'When the lad for longing sighs', who wants from the girl what will transfer to her the pains of love and leave him free of them. But the happy silence of lovers is fantasized in 'The Merry Guide' (*ASL*, xlii), a poem which Leavis used to choose in discussion classes as an example of all that was wrong with the by-then moribund tradition of Georgian pastoral poetry. It imagines a journey through a loved English landscape, not with Narcissus but with Mercury, the ideal companion and messenger of the gods:

> With lips that brim with laughter
> But never once respond,
> And feet that fly on feathers,
> And serpent-circled wand.

He is not only a messenger of love, but has himself the loved

one's longed-for features, knowledge and behaviour, with
nothing to explain:

> With mien to match the morning
>   And gay delightful guise
> And friendly brows and laughter
>   He looked me in the eyes.
>
> Oh whence, I asked, and whither?
>   He smiled and would not say,
> And looked at me and beckoned
>   And laughed and led the way.
>
> And with kind looks and laughter
>   And nought to say beside
> We two went on together,
>   I and my happy guide.

In one of the most moving—happily moving—poems in the
series, the poet who usually over-punctuates lets the verse
have its head, all its stiffness of precision flowing into the
easiest phrases—kind looks, laughter, friendly brows.

But the happy guide is also conductor of the dead, whom
the poem sees as giving the soul on its last journey all the
affection it could not receive in life. And with that all the
speechless fellow-feeling of the dead:

> And like the cloudy shadows
>   Across the country blown
> We two fare on for ever,
>   But not we two alone.
>
> With the great gale we journey
>   That breathes from gardens thinned,
> Borne in the drift of blossoms
>   Whose petals throng the wind;
>
> Buoyed on the heaven-heard whisper
>   Of dancing leaflets whirled
> From all the woods that autumn
>   Bereaves in all the world.
>
> And midst the fluttering legion
>   Of all that ever died
> I follow, and before us
>   Goes the delightful guide . . .

No wonder, perhaps, that Leavis disliked the poem, in which

he saw a facile sentiment supported by what—inspired by such poems as this—had become a 'This England' atmosphere of nestling church spires and weathered timbers. Leavis was discriminating about Georgian poetry, seeing Edward Thomas and Edmund Blunden as the two poets who justified its philosophy and manner, and sharply distinguishing their art, and that of Hardy, from the host of imitators and purveyors of cottage life and country weekend. But his distaste for 'The Merry Guide' must have been somewhat disingenuous if, as we can suspect, it was really for the unspoken love-relation in the poem. About this there is nothing sentimental. Housman puts a sad theme in a happy way, showing how the death guide, in whom we see all we can never have, accompanies us through life. Fulfilment in love comes only in the imagination of it.

Leavis was in sharp reaction against what he called 'the cult of T. E. Lawrence', the romantic and adventurous homosexual who was tacitly something of a hero to Housman, as he was so more openly to many others. The sharp reaction against such things among the intellectuals of the thirties is revealed in the record of a controversy which appeared in the *New Statesman* in 1936, at the time of Housman's obituaries, and was reprinted in 1945 in Cyril Connolly's *The Condemned Playground*. Strong feelings were exhibited on both sides. Housman, who when young had rejected the later Swinburne, and who studiously ignored the poets of his own era, would have enjoyed the controversy. He was himself very much aware how innovative he had been in his time, as the last poem in *A Shropshire Lad* shows, and the rejection of him by the new men would have given him neither surprise nor pain. But Leavis, not unlike Cyril Connolly who talked of Housman's 'Georgian sham-pastoral', seems to have accepted guilt by association, rather than giving his normally close and attentive reading to 'Reveille' or the 'The Merry Guide'. And Connolly went on to speak of 'popular trends—imperialism, place-nostalgia, games, beer—common to the poetry of the time'. He concluded that Housman had written 'some poems unworthy of Kipling and others unworthy of Belloc'.

Like Leavis, Connolly missed the point, supposing that Housman was being enthusiastic about the Empire, like

Kipling, or about the English countryside, like Belloc. But
enthusiasm was not Housman's state of mind, nor a dynamic
of his art. The poets of the time threw themselves heart and
soul into the good work, as it were, as if it were a cricket-
match. Their enthusiasm is open and eager, but also slightly
bogus and it was as alien to Housman as the languid airs of
the *fin-de-siècle* had been. Probably without conscious intention, 'The Merry Guide' sets up its own sort of parody of the
mode in which it appears to operate: parody of the inconspicuous and equivocal kind which came naturally to a
poet with a tacit aversion to poetical enthusiasm, and one to
whose creative nature it was natural to dissimulate:

> Oh whence, I asked, and whither?
> He smiled and would not say,

are lines which blend what might be appropriate to comic
verse with seriousness of a quite different sort. Like the guide
himself, with his 'gay regards of promise', these different tones
flit past in the poem with mysterious ease. About the beauties
of the poem—the 'valley-guarded granges' and 'sunstruck
vanes afield' there is nothing deliberately deep or 'heartfelt',
in the Georgian 'This England' sense; their sharp, graceful
accuracy is characteristically at variance with the descriptive
tone they imply. The poet is not taking us on a tour of
'designated areas of outstanding natural beauty' (how much
he would have disliked that categorization, and the thinking
behind it), and yet at the same time one can see just why
Leavis assumed Housman's lines were saying: 'Here is
poetical gold: take it! Here is radiant beauty; be moved.'
Leavis fell straight into a trap. A Shropshire Lad is full of them.
They come in many and ingenious kinds, and the verses
thread their way among them without ever seeming to be
aware they have put them in our path.

'Housman's proffer of his imagery is simple and simple-
minded . . . the reader takes in at a glance the value offered; it
is recognised currency; the beauty is conventional and
familiar.' Or was it Leavis who was being a bit simple-
minded? Certainly the poetry does not in the least object to
this account of it. It makes the brooks run gold and the
pastures glitter, and readers responded immediately; but still

they felt—obscurely they felt, as Blake's reader does—the sense of meaning that makes the hair stand up. But that was not the kind of meaning that Leavis, with his preference for a positively articulate and sophisticated collusion between poet and reader, was disposed to notice or comment upon. The fashion and idiom of their time, and its predetermination to find Housman the way they wanted, made critics as intelligent as Leavis and Connolly, whose tastes in other respects widely diverged, equally insensible to what actually goes on in *A Shropshire Lad*, and in the other poems.

'Bereaves' ('From all the woods that autumn | Bereaves in all the world') strikes an unexpected note—widows, orphans, pensions—in two lines that seem wholly evocative of pastoral plangency. The tone of the two lines does not confide in us, any more than his guide responds to the poet, even though 'the sadness of things', in the poetical sense, may seem to want the appearance of being summed up in them. The poem and its experience are 'delightful', the autumnal fall a part of it, and 'delightful' is a three-times-repeated word which carries its own quizzical charge, like the 'whence' and the 'whither', the 'lips that brim with laughter | But never once respond'.

The tone of the poem is so different from that of 'The winds out of the west land blow' (*ASL*, xxxviii), three poems before it, that a different kind of poet seems present there.

> The winds out of the west land blow,
> My friends have breathed them there;
> Warm with the blood of lads I know
> Comes east the sighing air.

It is indeed a different kind of poet; one who claims in this other fantasy that the wind from Shropshire is an emanation of his friends' voices, warm with their breath and blood, and that they 'made words of it with tongues | That talk no more to me'.

> Their voices, dying as they fly,
> Loose on the wind are sown;
> The names of men blow soundless by,
> My fellows' and my own.

A soundless wind is as metaphysical a concept as making tongues out of it, which turn to sighs in the friendless distance. Where 'The Merry Guide' is conscious and quizzical, with its key negative in 'lips that brim with laughter | But never once respond', and its mercurial vision graceful and pointed, this poem seems absorbed in listening to absent voices that really do respond. More than that, its rapt absorption in what to a metaphysical poet would be merely an effective conceit, shows Housman intent on his personal fantasy of a frank and free communication, in the Shropshire of the mind. Both poems are daydreams about comradeship, but the tone and feel of dream in each is utterly different.

It is this unpredictability which seemed to pass Leavis by, and in his own way Connolly too, for each took it for granted that Housman was the most predictable of poets, relying on a set of simple properties. 'The Merry Guide' and 'The winds out of the west land blows' show not only how various is the handling of these, but how variously Housman uses the conceit itself, and its manifestations. The spruceness of Mercury's gear, the 'feet that fly on feathers | And serpent-circled wand', have a slight and appropriate appearance of stage comedy, while the wind that blows in the second poem, carrying the names of men like dead leaves or scraps of paper, is as sad as nature, and as indeterminately passive. Housman originally wrote 'thick on the wind', and changed it to 'loose' in the 1923 edition, an alteration probably meditated for some time. It increases the poem's sense of helplessness and passivity, an atmosphere quite occluding the metaphysical machinery by which it is operated. The same thing happens in reverse in this poem:

> From far, from eve and morning
> And yon twelve-winded sky,
> The stuff of life to knit me
> Blew hither: here am I.
>
> Now—for a breath I tarry
> Nor yet disperse apart—
> Take my hand quick and tell me,
> What have you in your heart.
>
> Speak now, and I will answer;
> How shall I help you, say;
> Ere to the wind's twelve quarters
> I take my endless way.
>
> (*ASL*, xxxii)

From its opening, with a tense and almost clumsy repetition, this poem is engrossed in its urgent message, while 'The winds out of the west land blow' gives itself over to the emptiness of the wind. The lines here seem like rapid questions, but there are no interrogation marks, and 'What have you in your heart' means what you have in your heart. The poem is fated; the answer are known, and the help cannot be given; but the note of excellent urgency remains, overriding the fancy of the poem, and the Lucretian echo I referred to earlier.

In the tone of the key-words 'loose' and 'disperse', the two poems are at opposite poles, but more important is the concentration in them, which quite refutes Leavis's strictures about the 'poetical' in Housman, and the predictable. Even when he uses deliberately grand and sonorous language, as in 'Revolution' (*LP*, xxxvi), or extravagant conceits as in 'Reveille' (*ASL*, iv), the language is wholly subordinated to the attack of meaning, and the transmission of an under-meaning. Our satisfaction in 'Revolution' comes from the reader's need to concentrate very carefully, as the lines follow each other, on what is happening; and on the way in which their deliberate and exact elegance aids the reader both to do this and to be highly conscious meanwhile of the opulent and sinister slow-motion of the process described.

> West and away the wheels of darkness roll,
>   Day's beamy banner up the east is borne,
> Spectres and fears, the nightmare and her foal,
>   Drown in the golden deluge of the morn.
>
> But over sea and continent from sight
>   Safe to the Indies has the earth conveyed
> The vast and moon-eclipsing cone of night,
>   Her towering foolscap of eternal shade.
>
> See, in mid heaven the sun is mounted; hark,
>   The belfries tingle to the noonday chime.
> 'Tis silent, and the subterranean dark
>   Has crossed the nadir, and begins to climb.

Housman wrote the second and third verses early, possibly about the same time as 'Reveille', and added the first in 1922 to complete the poem for *Last Poems*. The air of instruction and command, incongrously coupled with luxuriant images, gives it something of the same air as 'Reveille'; but its title was added after its first publication, when Housman let the headmaster of Winchester have the poem for an anthology. He suggested the title might be of use, 'as most readers do not seem to see that it is a parable'.

A parable of what? Of change and progress? Of perpetual human optimism, and its perpetual destiny? But he hardly ever uttered a word about his poetry without implying a joke, or the enigmatic possibility of one; so it is unlikely that the title, or the 'parable', need be taken very seriously. The personal philosophy he called 'pejorism'—of things tending always to get rather worse—was probably intended as much as anything else to needle those of his own or a previous generation who thought of themselves as 'meliorists', like George Eliot, and even Hardy. I suspect that Housman may have planned some kind of reversal, as he often did, of pious or scriptural doctrine: possibly in this case the well-known Victorian hymn which rejoices that 'the voice of prayer is never silent', as light and dark succeed each other over earth's span. It is a hymn with memorable lines like 'while earth rolls onward into light', and a sardonic echo of it might have seemed to him not a bad idea for a school anthology. His 'parable' might be that darkness lay in wait every noon, prefiguring the final dark to come, and that 'Thy Church unsleeping' could do nothing about it. 'The golden deluge of the morn', in which it is bliss to be alive and baptized, inundates nightmares and their progeny in a reversal of the Flood. But they will return from under the water.

Nor is that the end of the parable. Like 'the silver dusk returning', the paradox of the golden deluge continues in a more homely metaphor, that of 'safe at home', or 'safe as houses', though here twinned with the exotic setting of the Indies. The earth is tender with the night, her eventual end and rest, and shepherds it with care on her diurnal round. Homeliness continues in the conceit of earth wearing her dark dunce's cap, a reversal of the paper one a mad poet or deluded scholar might have assigned it: for earth's cap is also a lady's headgear, a badge of status and repose. The opulence of the poem is both sardonic and comforting; but there is something in it too that goes against the uses of humour: 'yet night approaches; better not to stay'.

Behind, or beneath, the poem is a child's experience of things, put in the suavest adult language. The drowning of nightmare and foal is a brief exaltation, but a greater reassurance is the safe seclusion and return of night, and the comfort of bed, a comfort shot through before sleep with the delicious terror of ghost-story imaginings, of the something or somebody beginning to stir, climbing slowly out of the dark place. The poem is thoroughly cosy but precisely disturbing as well, containing, as so often with Housman's best, several interpretative versions of itself. Bland maturity and fastidious diction are set against the very real childlike fears and ecstasies conjured up, the tingle of intimate sensation against astronomic majesty. No poem of Housman's, not even 'Reveille', could better refute Leavis's contention that all we are offered is 'poetical gold'. Even the most conventional aspect of Housman's poetic diction, compounds like 'moon-eclipsing' and 'twelve-winded', are not decorative, but always intent on tracing a story and a meaning.

Nor is there anything in the least predictable about such a story. It goes inward too quickly and too far to do anything but surprise us, even when its span is so neatly drawn, as here, between age and childhood; the knowledge of extinction, and the cadence and sentiment of hymns that promise immortality, and dawns that lead on another day. At the end of 'The Name and Nature of Poetry', Housman referred to the last poem in *A Shropshire Lad*, and told the story of its composition—two stanzas as he walked on Hampstead Heath, one 'with a little coaxing after tea', one which had to be written 'thirteen times, and it was more than a twelvemonth before I got it right'. Naturally enough Housman did not reveal then, nor did he later, the order of composition. Characteristically he made a little mystery out of it, and although several admirers have made their speculations, most notably F. W. Bateson in the *Housman Society Journal* (1974), the riddle itself was more a question of publicity than of critical importance. But what it does indicate is something about the unexpectedness of Housman's poetic effects: their power to intrigue the reader by their casually careful abruptness, to lead him on and not to let him down. Philip Larkin observed of Emily Dickinson's poetry that she came to make a formula of first lines, brilliantly arresting openings which inspiration could not sustain, and which except in a handful of marvellous examples fell off into the incoherence which is her particular style of banality.* With typical modesty Larkin remarks about his own poems that in many cases the last line came to him first, 'and then it was just a matter of filling in'. That is another version of Housman's own sardonic objectivity; but it does seem true that both Dickinson and Larkin are more recognizably themselves in what they write—more confirmed in their own kinds of effect—than is the case with Housman. The more type-cast his mythology and methods might seem to be, the more further enquiry will show Housman evading the pattern, in complex and unexpected ways. The grounds of objection chosen by Leavis will be found to be just where the poetry is at its most unexpected and most original.

* *Required Writing*, 194.

CHAPTER 9

Strong Feelings

When Housman was a professor at London University he accepted a lunch invitation from Frank Harris and some of his journalist friends. They tried to flatter the author of *A Shropshire Lad* by praising 'the bitter sarcasm' of the first poem in it. This celebrates the Golden Jubilee of Queen Victoria in 1887, and ten years later Housman wrote a letter vividly describing the same Shropshire beacon fires, blazing for the Queen's Diamond Jubilee. Everyone who goes in for 'bitter sarcasm' takes a pride in themselves for doing so; and Frank Harris and his friends thought they recognized it in Housman's verse, in lines that used and misused the piety of the National Anthem—'Because 'tis fifty years to-night | That God has saved the Queen'—or the Scriptures—'The saviours come not home to-night: | Themselves they could not save.' From their own point of view they were right, but they did not recognize that what they thought of as sarcasm or irony here has an unexpected and heartfelt use. Housman uses the voice of sarcasm to make his point with a very special and personal simplicity and fervour, and also piety.

What was his reply to the attempted flattery? 'I never intended to poke fun, as you call it, at patriotism, and I can find nothing in the sentiment to make mockery of: I meant it sincerely; if Englishmen breed as good men as their fathers, then God will save their Queen.' And, according to Harris, Housman added 'precisely but with anger', 'I can only reject and resent your—your truculent praise'. Harris and his friends were no doubt amused at having both angered and discomposed the learned professor, for whom the 'Lads of the Fifty-third', the Shropshire Light Infantry, were a powerful, almost a sacred talisman in the poem placed at the front of his book:

> Now, when the flame they watch not towers
> About the soil they trod,

Lads, we'll remember friends of ours
Who shared the work with God.

To skies that knit their heartstrings right,
To fields that bred them brave,
The saviours come not home to-night:
Themselves they could not save.

Sharing with God the work of saving the Queen is an idea that
would have given the troops some amusement. What misled
Harris and his friends is the tone in which the poem contains
their own irreverence inside the reverence it feels for them. In
an essay Cleanth Brooks adds a slightly different point: 'A
pious sentiment, a patriotic cliché is suddenly taken seriously
and is made to work in a normal English sentence. It is as
shocking as if a bishop had suddenly used his crozier . . . to
lay hold upon a live sheep.'*

But the poem is indifferent to the idea of a shock, and to the
way the reader receives it. It is absent in its own kind of piety,
and in the fervour with which it remembers the absent ones:
'tombstones show | And Shropshire names are read; | And the
Nile spills his overflow | Beside the Severn's dead.' That swift
reference to the annually flooding Nile confirms that the poet's
eye is not on us, and also the way it passes up the point that
Harris and his friends would have relished: her soldiers
'saving' the Queen in these distant places, as if the troops in
Vietnam had been engaged in saving their president. A poet
today would take trouble to show his awareness of such
things, just as he would take care to make part of the poem a
simultaneous demonstration of the way it worked. But
Housman's poems have a long fuse, the gap between impact
and feeling, and implication, being prolonged almost in-
definitely.

In his introduction to the *Collected Poems and Selected Prose*,
Christopher Ricks observes that the poet can sometimes
resemble a textual scholar engaged in an act of editorial
imagination, putting an unexpected construction on the
material he glosses. Housman is, so to speak, conjecturing his
own text, making alive something that generations of scholars—

* In Christopher Ricks (ed.), *A. E. Housman: A Collection of Critical Essays* (London,
1968).

or public men in the case of the National Anthem—have left
for dead through their mechanical reverence. This is as
ingenious as it is suggestive, even though it misrepresents the
nature of the poems' original impact, and their lack of
collusion with the reader. It is a Lowell rather than a
Housman who edits and discusses inside the poems themselves the nature of his poems; and poets today cannot resist
seeing a poem as a workshop, or what Seamus Heaney has
called a TV replay, always enacting how its own goal was
scored. But in Housman's case the feelings and their
implications are still on explosive terms: the poet too
engrossed or disturbed to include his own commentary.

Frank Harris saw how disturbed he was, and was amused,
and recorded his amusement in his *Contemporary Portraits* for
the reader's benefit. It is quite likely that he also intuited
Housman's special relationship with soldiers: he would have
been familiar with men, not so unlike the professor of Latin,
who hung around the barracks and obtained their services, in
the same way that men like himself went after Soho
prostitutes. The poem that celebrates the Jubilee bonfires on
Clee ends on a different note:

> Oh, God will save her, fear you not:
>   Be you the men you've been,
> Get you the sons your fathers got,
>   And God will save the Queen.

But the fervour goes into the sentiment, not into its
expression: the two seem detached from each other, even at
odds, for just as there is no suggestion in the earlier verse
('Themselves they could not save') of deliberate and self-
conscious blasphemy, so there is none here of personal sexual
feeling. We are listening to something that came unbidden
into his head and speaks through him. This makes, as so often
with this poet, for a kind of spontaneous complexity. His
fervour is with the soldiers, yet he will not get sons as they do.
He is with them, but outside them. It is his feeling for the
'Fifty-third' that defamiliarizes piety and patriotism, and the
platitudes that surround them, in such a startling way. (Not
the least startling is the way in which Housman apparently
said 'their queen' to Harris, not 'the queen'.)

Propaganda even at their best, Kipling's poems about the troops try consciously and hard to avoid the obvious stigma of propaganda, but often make it more distasteful in the process. His soldiers don't go for patriotic cant, and despise the flag-flappers who proclaim it; they get on with the job and joke among their equals. As much of an outsider in his own fashion as Housman was, Kipling none the less proclaims his understanding of the troops' real and inner feelings. Housman can be just as emphatic, but the undercover habit of his poetry gives it both a genuine detachment and a correspondingly powerful identification with what it says and feels. He does not take his soldiers over, as Kipling does, and try to persuade us that he really knows them. His feelings are deeper, but they are not possessive or proprietary.

We see this in 'Epitaph on an Army of Mercenaries' (*LP*, xxxvii), which was published in *The Times* in October 1917, the third anniversary of the first Battle of Ypres, where the old professional British army had died. The form is borrowed from classical sources, but there is no parade of the laconic impassive, or of a literary antecedent. A mercenary soldier who fought for hire was a not dishonourable figure in the Hellenistic and Roman world; and the term itself has been in continuous use, from the days when unpaid mercenaries nearly sacked an ungrateful Carthage to the local wars of our own time. Richard Wilbur remarks, after pointing out the classical overtones, that the poem hardly needs them but depends more on the Miltonic echo.* This could be said to be at the expense of the orthodox and the *bien pensants*, who assume that God will always defend the right. Not God's angels but mercenary troops have done this, and the foundations that were rocked in Milton's epic stand as solid as ever. The detachment of the epitaph on those who 'saved the sum of things for pay' is oddly presumptive of the reader's ignorance. The reader may be surprised by the way in which the poet presents an unusual way of looking at the British army as if that way were perfectly familiar, in the same way that he had presented that army's achievement in saving 'their queen'. Housman takes for granted that his reader sees his own army as an army of mercenaries, even though he may

* In Ricks (ed.), *A. E. Housman: A Collection of Critical Essays.*

not be familiar with the history of mercenaries and their calling. But no propaganda is involved. The poem is not saying: 'Aren't you ashamed to be defended by mercenaries, for whom earning the meagre pay you give them is more important than saving the wealth of civilization?' The poem instantly impresses and surprises; and our curiosity about what has caused this takes us, as it were, calmly into history and legend, and back to the present.

Yet the emotion in the poem is as strongly latent as it is in '1887', the Queen's Jubilee poem which opened *A Shropshire Lad*. The past is used much more effectively, according to the way Housman's best poetry works, than it is in the poem's near neighbour, 'The Oracles' (*LP*, xxv) which was written after the Boer War. Here the classical background is peremptory, a trifle laboured. There are no more oracles in Greece, of the sort who spoke through the wind in the grove, the clang of bronze vessels, and the murmur of the fountain. But one oracle still remains: 'The heart within, that tells the truth and tells it twice as plain.' Housman here comes near to putting on his sardonic-exaggerative cap, as he does in 'The chestnut casts his flambeaux' (*LP*, ix), inflating the tone expression-lessly, but deliberately. This inner oracle he addresses as 'my lass', and he can rely on her accuracy when she tells him 'That she and I should surely die and never live again'. The last stanza expands the point with a fine bravura:

The King with half the East at heel is marched from lands of morning;
*   Their fighters drink the rivers up, their shafts benight the air,*
And he that stands will die for nought, and home there's no returning.
   The Spartans on the sea-wet rock sat down and combed their hair.

Interestingly, Housman wrote to a friend that 'I do not admire the oracle poem as much as some people do. The italics, as elsewhere, are equivalent to inverted commas, and give the supposed words of the oracle.' It is true that Housman can in his own way be as reticent when he raises his voice as when he speaks quietly, but the true laconic touch can hardly be got in a metre more suited to a patriotic poem by Sir Henry Newbolt. It is better to take for granted that a good soldier wins nothing for himself by dying, than to have the heart proclaim it as stridently as the Pythoness.

Yet the contrast between the celebrated last line, and what has gone before, is highly effective. Christopher Ricks has pointed out the significance of another such contrast, in the poem 'I to my perils | Of cheat and charmer' (*MP*, vi), which 'says a dour glum cramping thing, but how does it say it? With wit and gaiety that are, if you like, utterly inappropriate. Instead of the "steady" tramp of military fortitude, there is the exquisite interlacing of a dance.'*

> I to my perils
>> Of cheat and charmer
>> Came clad in armour
>> By stars benign.
> Hope lies to mortals
>> And most believe her,
>> But man's deceiver
>> Was never mine.
>
> The thoughts of others
>> Were light and fleeting,
>> Of lovers' meeting
>> Or luck or fame.
> Mine were of trouble,
>> And mine were steady,
>> So I was ready
>> When trouble came.

Although Ricks gives excellent reasons for admiring it, the poem itself does not seem quite to live up to that admiration. This may be because it admires itself too much, its own deft movement and 'inappropriate' gaiety. Housman excluded it from *Last Poems*, though he kept in 'The Oracles', and perhaps he came to feel distaste for the rather calculating element of showing off in both. Such effects of contrast are best in him when they are much less showy, as in 'Spring Morning' (*LP*, xvi). (The banality of Housman's occasional titles is one of their more discreet charms.)

> Now the scorned unlucky lad
> Rousing from his pillow gnawn
> Mans his heart and deep and glad
> Drinks the valiant air of dawn.

* In Ricks (ed.), *A. E. Housman: A Collection of Critical Essays.*

Those great yawning vowel sounds are in subtle relationship with the disciplined bustle of getting up and resuming the routine, a more expressive relationship than that suggested in 'I to my perils', where the dance is very deliberately directed to the concluding pirouette of biblical and home-brewed wisdom. It is certainly ingenious—the trouble that came to Job among his normal adversities is pre-empted by Housman's reversal of the saying about not meeting trouble half-way— but such ingenuity is secured here at the expense of feeling: the most important thing, however much he may seem to avoid procuring it.

Hardy's last collection of poems, *Winter Words*, contains one of three stanzas entitled 'He never expected much or A Consideration, on my eighty-sixth birthday'. The world addresses the poet:

> 'I do not promise overmuch,
>   Child; overmuch;
> Just neutral-tinted haps and such,'
>   You said to minds like mine.
> Wise warning for your credit's sake!
> Which I for one failed not to take,
> And hence could stem such strain and ache
>   As each year might assign.

Hardy makes the same point as Housman, not as if striking up a tune but in his ordinary voice. He and the world are on familiar terms from way back.

> 'Twas then you said, and since have said,
>   Times since have said . . .

The words convey the monotony of the relation; and also the complacency of the shrewd operator who 'owns' that he never expected life to be 'all fair'. In the twin stanzas of 'I to my perils' Housman is not himself at all, but a performer in a style of which he knows himself to be a virtuoso. His stanzas seem to know and reveal this in an engaging way, not as if the author were wearing a Yeatsian mask but as if he were consciously being poetical in a certain style, perhaps for the writing of parodies or nonsense poetry. It is the same mode that he makes play with at the end of *A Shropshire Lad* (*ASL*, lxii), 'Terence, this is stupid stuff', and in the stanzas his brother printed as an epigraph for *More Poems*, 'They say my verse is sad: no wonder . . .' The former presents the poet, not as the dancing man of 'Mine were of trouble, | And mine were steady', but in the guise of Mithridates, the king who reigned in the east, and who was said to have accustomed himself by degrees to every poison 'From the many-venomed earth':

> First a little, thence to more,
> He sampled all her killing store;
> And easy, smiling, seasoned sound,
> Sate the king when healths went round.

The image of Housman as smiling monarch, courtly host, is both droller and more penetratingly incongruous, in the context of human woes, than is the man who treads the measure with cheat and charmer. Neither foes nor loving friends can hurt him, and the imagined discomfiture of both gives him the pleasure that makes the poem.

Housman and Hardy are temperamentally akin in many ways, and chiefly in their mode of survival. Reluctance to be alive becomes itself a way of living, and of doing it with industry and determination. 'Childhood among the Ferns' is about the very young Hardy who sat snug in a green cave under the bracken in the rain,

> And queried in the green rays as I sate
> 'Why should I have to grow to man's estate,
> And this afar-noised World perambulate?'

Housman, a knowledgeable botanist while still in his teens, would not have commented with Hardy's literalness on the bracken cave, and the fear in it of the grown-up world to come. But he too could be literal about nature in his own way, as in 'Far in a western brookland | That bred me long ago' (*ASL*, lii), in which he imagines a Heine-like wanderer in the country where he was born:

> There, in the windless night-time,
>   The wanderer, marvelling why,
> Halts on the bridge to hearken
>   How soft the poplars sigh.
>
> He hears: no more remembered
>   In fields where I was known,
> Here I lie down in London
>   And turn to rest alone.

Housman knew that poplars, the black poplar especially, have
a faint leaf crepitation in the calmest weather; and he was
memorably scornful about the artist his publisher employed in
later days who did an illustration showing the conventional
pointed trees bowing in a brisk gale. 'The wanderer marvel-
ling why' does not know that poplars whisper, and Housman
makes an adroit use of that fact to personify his own unquiet
soul, following on an echo of Sappho's lines about lying alone
in the night:

> There, by the starlit fences,
>   The wanderer halts and hears
> My soul that lingers sighing
>   About the glimmering weirs.

With both Hardy and Housman the sharpness of the fact and
the authenticity of the recollection contrasts with the self-
comforting emotion involved. On occasion Housman employs
an unusual turn of syntax, not with Hardy's deliberate oddity
but with something of his homeliness, to give this 'comfort' a
kind of hard, private gusto. 'Mithridates, he died old' . . . But
the feeling is quite different, and its impact far greater, when
he uses the same syntactic turn in this poem:

> It nods and curtseys and recovers
>   When the wind blows above,
> The nettle on the graves of lovers
>   That hanged themselves for love.

> The nettle nods, the wind blows over,
>   The man, he does not move,
> The lover of the grave, the lover
>   That hanged himself for love.
>
>   (*ASL*, xvi)

Repetition in the sentence structure blends with the nettle's
repeated movement, and in the almost quaint incredulity of
'The man, he does not move'. Surprise has never been more
quietly or emptily expressed.

   In the volume of essays he edited Ricks makes some
interesting points about this famous poem, as do Randall
Jarrell and F. W. Bateson, who differ about the sense of
'recover'. The word as used here by Housman is cited in the
OED as exemplifying an eighteenth-century usage: that of

return to the vertical after the act of bowing or 'courtseying'. But from this Jarrell assumes that the nettle is executing a dance on the grave, the formal movement of a minuet; while Bateson, more literally, points out that a rooted plant can do no more than incline itself from the vertical. While recognizing Bateson's objection, Housman as textual critic might reasonably have pointed out that the poet employing the anthropomorphic convention can do as he pleases in its context. No matter for its roots, the nettle may be imagined as going through the formal motions of a dance, although Ricks is surely misleading in continuing to rub in his point about Housman's habitual and straight-faced blasphemy—would it not be an act of extreme discourtesy, he asks, to dance on a grave? This is surely not what the reader intuits, or the impression he receives; the poem's gentleness and vacancy expressly contradict any idea of a conscious performance, whether by the nettle that moves, or the man who does not. Bateson remarks that the verse stanza is about hanged lovers in general, but in the repetition that follows 'the plurals have become singulars'. The third and fourth lines of the first verse express a quite, so to speak, cheery concept; it picturesquely applies to a lot of unfortunates past and present, with whose fate we are not specially concerned. But 'the man' in the second verse is our man, the one whose grave and nettles are now before the eyes of poet and reader.

Housman is a specialist in using clichés in an unexpected context, or the wrong way round, in order to defamiliarize them into making a startling point. 'The put to death, the perished nation' has not been massacred by a tyrant, or dealt with by the hangman, but the fate and end of its people are the same. 'A dead man out of mind' is out of sight and out of mind, and the second because the first: he has gone one further than Hardy's 'spectral manikin', who lives briefly and precariously in the thought of others. 'The nation that is not' has no more existence than lies have—the things which are not. Housman is 'blasphemous' because he is so familiar with the speech of the Bible and the Prayer Book that he uses them in any context, and for all purposes. Feeling sinks deep in when he does this; or when he uses, almost invisibly, a common word in different senses:

> Around the huddling homesteads
>   The leafless timber roars,
> And the dead call the dying
>   And finger at the doors.
> Oh, yonder faltering fingers
>   Are hands I used to hold;
> Their false companion drowses
>   And leaves them in the cold.
>   (*LP*, xix)

To be 'left in the cold' is the term for those who have failed to find a place on the social scene, or fit in on an amorous one. Here it is the literal fate of the dead. But more noticeable are the different senses in which the word 'fingers' occurs, as verb and noun. The verb is used in a sinister and literary sense, sinister because it is literary. Ghosts in ballad and story finger at doors, crying to be let in; but these are the hands of friends or lovers, their touch once loving and firm and companionable. Between verb and noun the sense switches abruptly. Dead men's fingers become alive and warm again in the minds of those who are dying because in the midst of life.

'In midnights of November' (*LP*, xix) is a good example of Housman mixing his different poetic ingredients together, but it does not entirely come off as a poem, and one sees why it was left uncompleted at the time of *A Shropshire Lad*, then thought to be of a standard good enough to be put in final form for 'New Poems' (as Housman often inadvertently referred to the collection he chose to call *Last Poems*). It is moving in its parts, but lacks the swift coherence and tension of his best; it has not quite digested, as most of the *Shropshire Lad* poems so successfully have, its own literary properties.

> In midnights of November,
>   When Dead Man's Fair is nigh,
> And danger in the valley,
>   And anger in the sky,

refers to the late-year fair held at Church Stretton by the Long Mynd, whose hills and sudden hollows could be dangerous to revellers returning home. But this piece of folklore from the Shropshire guide, highly effective in poems like 'The Welsh Marches' (*ASL*, xxviii) seems at odds with the intimacy of this poem, its deep physical longing for comrades or brothers now dead. The haunting sense of communion in death is more haunting still in poems Housman never published, and which appeared in *More Poems*:

> Because I liked you better
> Than suits a man to say,
> It irked you, and I promised
> To throw the thought away.

Liking and *irking* join in the same understatement. The thought, like a stiff suit that doesn't fit, cramps a man and is better thrown away. The manuscript of 'Shake hands, we shall never be friends, all's over' (*MP*, xxx) remained incomplete, and all the more touching because it seems to fail from its own emotion to make the same neat point as its successor, in which 'the lad that loved you' has kept his word to forget that love, because he is dead. It cannot help but hope for a situation in which the lover may render some longed-for service:

> But if you come to a road where danger
> Or guilt or anguish or shame's to share,
> Be good to the lad that loves you true
> And the soul that was born to die for you
> And whistle and I'll be there.

It is one of Housman's most moving poems, but even here wistfulness and vulnerability retain their sharpness. 'The soul that was born to die for you' glances not only at the supreme Christian sacrifice, but at the more sardonic thought that an immortal soul can be predestined to die from love. It was born not to save but to die from the wish to do so. Danger, guilt, shame, and anguish might well have attended their love, had it been mutual; but if the loved one should ever find such troubles on his own, the lover would ask nothing better than to take them on himself. The thought is certainly wistful, for Moses Jackson had other things to do and to think of than the poet who would have made such a sacrifice. And the poem, too, knows that an importunate lover is irksome, no matter what sacrifice he wishes to make—indeed because he wishes to make them. 'Oh whistle and I'll come to you, my lad' is the refrain of a country ballad, and of a girl who will sacrifice family and friends at any time to join her lover. She will come

like a dog to its master. But by coincidence it is also the title of
a famous ghost story by Housman's friend, contemporary,
and fellow-scholar, M. R. James, in which the whistle has a
different consequence, for something spectral and menacing
hears and attends from beyond the grave.

The devoted lover may also be the demon lover; or perhaps
envisage himself, affectionately or sardonically, in that light.
A poem, possibly written about the same time, elaborates the
idea:

> Crossing alone the nighted ferry
>   With the one coin for fee,
> Whom, on the wharf of Lethe waiting,
>   Count you to find? Not me.
>
> The brisk fond lackey to fetch and carry,
>   The true, sick-hearted slave,
> Expect him not in the just city
>   And free land of the grave.
>
> (MP, xxiii)

In a brilliant analysis, Randall Jarrell points out that this
terse little poem works two ways.* The grave is just and free
because love, with all its humiliations and burdens, counts
there for nothing. On the other hand how could the grave, in
which there is no space and nothing happens, be described as
a land and a city? By colliding the vacancy of the grave with
the populous imagined world of Hades, Housman gives his
own version of the Greek Anthology epigram in which a dead
man tells a living one that Hades and Pluto are all a fable, but
if he'd rather hear something different, why then, in hell there
are fat oxen on sale for a penny.

Jarrell concludes that 'this particular-seeming little poem
turns out to be general enough', full of implicit attitudes
'toward love, life, and death'. That is true, but more
important for the poem's success is the game being played
with the idea. So far from being the concentratedly sardonic,
and even venomous, affair read by Jarrell, the poem seems to
me to have as well something relaxed about it, cheerfully
good-natured, as if the poet were sharing the joke in his

---

* In Ricks (ed.), *A. E. Housman: A Collection of Critical Essays*.

question with the friend to whom he is speaking. 'Not me',
'count me out', are the sort of comments, jovially made, once
customary among the young men who 'chaffed' each other,
and whose company meant so much to the poet. The idea of
waiting on the platform of Hades to meet such a friend is one
that gives him a special amusement. I won't be hovering
around you down there, as I have been here in Bayswater,
where, as a young man, Housman had shared a flat with the
Jackson brothers.

A kind of humour is the keynote, coming not only from the
incongruity of the imagined situation but from the inter-
changeability of sexual roles. A member of either sex might be
there, clutching the coin like a bus-fare, and expecting the
faithful partner, to whom he or she used to offer a cheek in an
unequal master–slave relation, to be waiting at the terminus.
Rupert Brooke wrote a poem, at perhaps about the same time,
in which he imagined an escape from famous *amours*. 'What
Paris was telling for good-bye to Helen | As he bundled her
into the train' was, 'it's not going to happen again, old
girl | It's not going to happen again.' 'Bundle' does more
obviously the same job as Housman's 'count'; but whereas
Brooke's word for the end of a famous relationship is comic,
Housman's is not so much bitter as deeply touching. Jarrell's
point is important too: the two concluding lines are necessarily self-deceiving. The slave thinks he has come to the land
of personal freedom and social justice, but the grave has the
last word.

In the case of 'Crossing alone the nighted ferry', Archie
Burnett's scholarship has revealed a text full of unresolved
variants. There are many versions of the adjectives in the
second stanza, one of which is 'prim'. The text Laurence
Housman decided on for *More Poems* is largely arbitrary. But
this is clearly not the case with 'Tarry, delight' (*MP*, xv), a
little masterpiece about the love of Hero and Leander. As with
the preceding examples, the device on which the poem rests is
the contrast between what is literary, sardonic, and predictable, and an undertone of personal longing and deep
emotional reciprocity:

> Tarry, delight, so seldom met,
>   So sure to perish, tarry still;

Forbear to cease or languish yet,
　　Though soon you must and will.

By Sestos town, in Hero's tower,
　　On Hero's heart Leander lies;
The signal torch has burnt its hour
　　And sputters as it dies.

Beneath him, in the nighted firth,
　　Between two continents complain
The seas he swam from earth to earth
　　And he must swim again.

The opening recalls, as if accidentally, an English lute song; and perhaps too the repetition of 'tarry' in Cressida's morning words to her lover Troilus in Shakespeare's play ('You men will never tarry . . . And then you would have tarried'). 'Nighted'—'the nighted ferry'—is a word Housman was clearly fond of; and 'firth' unites the tale from the Hellespont with northern places. (Byron, who used to pride himself on swimming Leander's route, learnt to swim in Aberdeen.) 'Sputters', too, has the down-to-earthness of a northern ballad, like the earth-to-earth swim which will make a grave for the doomed young man. The image of lying on Hero's heart is moving in its matter-of-factness, the delight so softly wooed in the opening lines. As with other seemingly spontaneous openings—'From far, from eve and morning', or 'Stars, I have seen the fall'—it has the air of a sudden break-out, an informal confidence. Here it makes the tone seem musing and preoccupied, and gives an absent note, intimate and gentle, to the formal hardness of the narration. In poems like these Housman shows his range, and a depth of craftsmanship as well as of controlled and detached feeling. The gap between detachment and feeling can produce a deliberative, even disquieting, impression of humour; and I shall say more about this in the next chapter.

CHAPTER 10

Jokes

Humour is the result of incongruity, usually an undeclared one. Short as they are, Housman's poems have plenty of these, as in this, from *More Poems*:

> Half-way, for one commandment broken,
>   The woman made her endless halt,
> And she to-day, a glistering token,
>   Stands in the wilderness of salt.
> Behind, the vats of judgment brewing,
>   Thundered, and thick the brimstone snowed;
> He to the hill of his undoing
>   Pursued his road.
>
> (MP, xxv)

One of Anna Akhmatova's poems commemorates the same occasion, and makes the point that Lot's wife was not foolish, or to be blamed, for turning to have a last look at 'the red towers of Sodom', and the house in which she had lived and been loved and borne children. The poet would have done the same. Housman too literalizes his story by reflecting on it; and in both cases reflection all takes place before the poem comes into being. One commandment—what is that? There are nine others: but the quiet emphasis on 'one' is itself a comment on divine justice. The victim of an endless halt is a comrade of all those who tread an endless road. Her lot is the lot of man, the silent pun in a poem which names no names. So much for Lot's wife—what about the man himself, and the cities of the plain? Wifeless, Lot took to the hills, but that did not help him, for in order to bear the seed of their tribe his daughters made him drunk and lay with him. His undoing was decreed and involuntary, like that of those who fall in love as Housman had. He must have liked the matter-of-fact way in which this part of the Bible takes sexual matters for granted, and tells of the girls offered to the Sodomites in place of the guest angels they desire. Housman would certainly have known the limerick current in his own Oxford college, about the young man of St John's who had sexual designs on the swans.

> But up came the porter
> Saying 'Here, take my daughter,
> Them swans are reserved for the dons.'

The crude humour that Housman enjoyed in later life was perhaps more common among middle-aged men than with clean-limbed, healthy undergraduates. But it lurks beneath the surface of his poems, making just the right loaded and incongruous contrast with the poetry's propriety; lurking here even in the spruce but inconspicuous dissyllabic rhymes, which are like those in the more accomplished kind of limerick. 'The vats of judgment', itself a metaphor full of incongruity, suggests wholesome things like beer-brewing; and the brimstone snowing, even as the vats brew, suggests, rather than any special demonstration of divine wrath, the one-damn-thing-after-another pattern of ordinary existence. Lot might have said with Job: 'I was not in safety, neither had I rest, neither was I quiet; yet trouble came.' The end of the poem is moving for the way it presses bleakly on, its patience at variance with what has happened before and after. Often in Housman's poetry the jest is, as it were, told to shut up.

There is the same kind of unassuming and rather chastening dignity in Housman's natural use of Bible language. In the soberness of what he says the joke of blasphemy has quite ceased to work. Ricks stresses the 'eisell and gall' with which Housman shoots the darts of the wicked from behind 'the calculated inoffensiveness of his verse-forms'. But blasphemy is a serious business, and Housman's humour evades it, just as it evades making the kind of heartfelt and 'touching' point in the Lot poem that Akhmatova makes in hers. The simplicity and violence of blasphemy, as practised by a Baudelaire or a Swift, is apt to be self-limiting: Housman's is less strident and more pervasive. The full vigour of his wit went into his letters and commentaries, where it is much more spectacular, but in the end less effective and less interesting. It is amusing, certainly, and must have amused the recipient, when Housman writes to his publisher that it would be as inappropriate to include his poems in a Nineties anthology as it would be to bring Lot into a book about Sodomites, 'in saying which I am not saying a word against sodomy, nor implying that intoxication and incest are in any way preferable'. That air of affected toleration seems demure enough, but it is highly obvious, and the humour in Housman's best poetry is not obvious at all.

It is true that his verse at its second-best can also be heavy-handed, and in the matter of wit as well. 'Ho, everyone that thirsteth | And hath the price to give' (*MP*, xxii), is even rather daring in its injunction to drink 'the stolen waters', which are death in scripture but life to the body and soul of the deprived young man. It was, in a sense, a genuine Nineties touch to urge the licence of desire, even in so laconic a style:

> It shall not last for ever,
>   No more than earth and skies;
> But he that drinks in season
>   Shall live before he dies.

Housman himself would not have published that poem, just as he would not have published 'Shake hands, we shall never be friends' (*MP*, xxx), with its reference to 'the soul that was born to die for you'. Although it seems eminently natural, even domestic, both that the lover should drink stolen waters and take for granted that he came on earth to perform the function claimed for Christ, the take-over draws attention to itself too openly, and this must be partly the reason why the poems were put away in the poet's lifetime.

The open poems of *A Shropshire Lad*, on the other hand, sometimes use Greek myth as domestically as they do the scriptures. One makes a strikingly intimate use of the myth of Narcissus, the writer imagining himself as one of the beautiful youth's victims, and advising him not to look into his eyes, for fear of seeing his own beauty there.

> Look not in my eyes, for fear
>   They mirror true the sight I see,
> And there you find your face too clear
>   And love it and be lost like me.
> One the long nights through must lie
>   Spent in star-defeated sighs,
> But why should you as well as I
>   Perish? gaze not in my eyes.
>   (*ASL*, xv)

The marvellous verse gives no hint of bitterness at all. The
question asked is almost suspiciously bland, as is the lilt which
tempers the quiet emphasis on the word 'one'. Fate written in
the stars has not crossed this love but doomed it before it
begins; but it is impossible not at least to imagine the joys of
mutuality.

> Delight it is in youth and May
>   To see the morn arise,
> And more delight to look all day
>   A lover in the eyes.
>   (*MP*, xviii)

A metaphysical poet might have made a conceit out of 'Look
not in my eyes', an open conceit which in Marvell or Crashaw
would not be afraid of extending its ingenuity into the
grotesque. Housman's tone is private, and tender, because the
joke is shared only between two non-lovers, for whom (or at
least for one of them) a shared joke will be the nearest thing to
love's intimacy. It is highly comical that you might chance to
look in my eyes and fall in love with your own image; and then
the pair of us would be in the same plight, both together and
apart. If you were Narcissus the added absurdity is that you
would never stop gazing, until you became like the dark-eyed
flower at the water's edge. And to have brought that about
would be an odd fate for me, even odder than the one I have.

It is a love poem which imagines two people, one
indifferent, sharing the joke two lovers might have at the
moment of discovering each other. And the tone is both tender
and tough—tender to the other but hard on himself, knowing
the joke's on him. The effect of intimacy lies in its being
almost unnoticeable, having its own sort of discretion.
Housman is adept at concealing the intimate behind the
obvious:

> Send me now, and I shall go;
>   Call me, I shall hear you call;
> Use me ere they lay me low
>   Where a man's no use at all;
>   (*ASL*, xxiv)

The poem hides its inner shrinking self behind its urgent note
and form. 'Here am I, man: now's your time' could be almost

intimidating, like 'Use me', but both conceal a real and plaintive longing, a feminine wish for a feminine role. The longing can be hidden by a tougher query—what use am I alive anyway?—but the incongruity between feelings persists and makes a secret comedy, quite different from the one set up by the poet with his friends, or his public, in the last two poems of A *Shropshire Lad*, where Mithridates ('First a little, thence to more') deliberately immunizes himself against human ills; or the poet takes trouble to prepare his verses, like flowers, for market, and then finds they are not in fashion.

Jokes can be the liveliest part of life, particularly when they invoke death. Observing that 'creation of life has no place in the universe of Housman', Edmund Wilson brought together a rather incongruous trio—'Alice and the Shropshire Lad and Marius the Epicurean'—in his contention that they 'are all the beings of a looking-glass world, either sexless or with an unreal sex which turns only towards itself in the mirror of art'.* One sees what he is getting at, and the same general point is made from a different angle by F. R. Leavis, in his view of the good Lawrentian artist as 'a whole man', whose art shows us how to separate the 'life' from the 'death' world. Wilson makes no pretence of pursuing his argument into the detail of Housman's poetry, for like Leavis's it is based on a general moral impression. Neither critic goes for humour, and Wilson ignores the fact that a life/death antithesis, in so far as it has any meaning at all in Housman's art, has its meaning in terms of a joke. Humour was Housman's mode of participating in life, and of sharing the confidence and the joke, in his own peculiar way, with others in the same boat. Comparing Housman with T. E. Lawrence, Wilson quotes the passage from *The Seven Pillars of Wisdom* which Housman had seen in a review and marked with the words 'This is me'. This passage in Lawrence is embarrassing to read now—the careful finicky style is very solemn—but Housman must at once have seen the point of what it said. It was about the terrible difficulty of communicating—by implication with those one might love and be loved by—and the horror of trying to 'open myself friendly to another'.

* Ricks (ed.), *A. E. Housman: A Collection of Critical Essays.*

The phrase itself has something sticky about it, and *Seven Pillars* is very much a book of its time and culture, revealing rather helplessly to us now the local characteristics which a later age can identify. By comparison Housman is not for an age but for all time, as Dryden said of Shakespeare; and one thing that has kept his poems fresh is the visible and not so visible fun in them. The mode by which Housman communicates himself is wholly different from the one attempted by T. E. Lawrence. If the poet Gray never 'spoke out', as Matthew Arnold regretted, it was because he had no need to: his 'Elegy' does it for him, in a way he could never have done himself. The diction of the 'Elegy' is itself a mode of intimacy, and although it may seem a conventionally eighteenth-century mode of diction it is none the less peculiarly Gray's own. So it is with Housman. His mode of speech is quite undated because wholly singular, whereas the idiom of T. E. Lawrence in *Seven Pillars* now seems that of his set, and of his time.

Humour is identical with singularity and has a close relation with what is personally stylized. For example, the peculiar use of bawdy words in Larkin's poetry has an effect of singularity, because 'piss' or 'sod' in that context are words that seem neither thoughtlessly crude, nor carefully self-conscious, but a natural part of his poetic being. In much the same way, Auden managed to make slogans, clichés, and political catchwords of the Thirties sound like one of his poetry's own personal trade-marks, giving it a kind of undercover individuality and fun. So again it is with Housman. The communicative ability in his verse makes an obvious contrast with the lack of it in the man. As he grew older the problem no doubt got less; and one reason why we may intuit that the later poems are not so urgent and explosive as the earlier ones is because they are more genial but less immediately intimate, and therefore less funny. The comparatively expansive Housman of later years is not the Housman whose poems make jokes.

Even that we cannot be sure of, because of the difficulty of dating. He could be both secretive and forgetful about when poems were written, remarking late in life that writing them was 'either easy or impossible'. Perhaps it is the 'easy' ones that are also most naturally funny; the later ones more obviously urbane? But the collusion of humour, its nearly intangible intimacy, may be present in the simplest and slightest of them:

> With rue my heart is laden
>   For golden friends I had,
> For many a rose-lipt maiden
>   And many a lightfoot lad.
>
> By brooks too broad for leaping
>   The lightfoot boys are laid;
> The rose-lipt girls are sleeping
>   In fields where roses fade.
>
> (ASL, liv)

It is a poem that has attracted few comments, and they are apt to be unfavourable. The poet John Crowe Ransom thought that even in verses of such classic and simple brevity something had gone wrong.* There seems to be confusion between the Elysian Fields and our pastoral earth—where are the sleepers supposed to be? Are the boys beside the Styx and the girls at home in the churchyard? In a way Ransom may have been right that something is wrong, but it may be the wrong note that sets the poem vibrating, as does the quiet switch from the maiden and lad of the first verse to the girls and boys of the second. The collective suicides in the first stanza of 'It nods and curtseys' (*ASL*, xvi), the nettle-on-the-grave poem, change equally quietly to the single victim of the second—'the man, he does not move'.

L. P. Wilkinson made the point, defending Housman against Cyril Connolly's criticisms, that the friends are 'golden' here in the sense in which both Greek and Latin writers used the term to describe a relationship of affection or love.† Shakespeare's golden lads and girls may carry this secondary sense too, although it has the primary meaning of rich or well-endowed, in contrast to the chimney-sweepers. Echoes of English girls and boys coming out to play, as well as of Heine, contrast with the classic lad and maiden. More important to the slightly cryptic nature of the poem's

---

* *The Southern Review*, 6 (1940).

† Ricks (ed.), *A. E. Housman: A Collection of Critical Essays*.

simplicity is the seemingly different fate of girls and boys. Death for one sex is as vigorous as an act of love, sharpened in the connotations of 'laid' and 'leaping', or like an athlete's gallant try at a feat impossible to perform. Death for boys is a climax of glorious failure, but for the girls it is different. Roses fade as their lips did in life, even though (*ASL*, xix) the laurel for the athlete's brows may wither more quickly. They seem still alive and fading in the marriage-bed of the grave. Sadness for them is the gradualness of age and decay; and the dying fall of the last two lines succeeds the curious elation with which the poet celebrates what seems the quick, clean death of the boys.

'With rue my heart is laden' is a caressingly inexpressive line, with a cadence more like Mörike than Heine, but the inexpressiveness shows something is afoot. As so often with Housman a world of comedy—even nonsense or play—is well concealed by convention. It is the opposite effect to his startled, excited, or preoccupied openings—'From far, from eve and morning' and 'Stars, I have seen them fall'—which seem to stumble over their own haste to come out:

> The sigh that heaves the grasses
>   Whence thou wilt never rise
> Is of the air that passes
>   And knows not if it sighs.
>
> The diamond tears adorning
>   Thy low mound on the lea,
> Those are the tears of morning,
>   That weeps, but not for thee.
>   (*LP*, xxvii)

This is more pointedly demure than 'With rue may heart is laden'. As Empson pointed out in *Some Versions of Pastoral*, we are so accustomed by verse to the Pathetic Fallacy that we assume morning must be weeping for something or someone, if not for us. Impassively the poet allows the words he chooses to reinforce one now exploded Pathetic Fallacy with another wider one, in the same way that he allows morning to associate itself with mourning. (George Barker makes a cruder use of the same pun in his sonnet on his mother, who will move 'from mourning into morning'; but Housman's own puns can be crude enough at times, as in his association of flowers 'lying about the world' with lovers who persuade the girl into the wood, where 'I will tell you lies').

Some of Housman's subtly and effectively humorous poems are also what might be called 'no-nonsense' poems of a recognizably English romantic kind, and a kind that also goes back through Keats, Byron, and Burns to Shakespeare. The pleasure in such poems is the combining spontaneously, as if in a live personality, the 'nonsense' of touching and beautiful expression with the 'no-nonsense' of seeing through it; but doing this in such a way that the two merge into one and are indissoluble. Housman said about 'Take O take those lips away' that it is nonsense, but 'ravishing poetry'. In fact his ear for vibrations must have detected that it combines 'nonsense' with 'no-nonsense', the charm of its utterance with the underlying sturdy if shabby wish to have those kisses returned, like jewels or rings: one's property rescued from an infatuation. In the Narcissus poem, 'Look not in my eyes' (*ASL*, xv), the same sort of thing is happening; and the imperative of the opening phrase echoes Shakespeare's sad love-song, while the words unfold a message at once dis-enchanted and still intimately affectionate. 'But why should you as well as I | Perish? gaze not in my eyes.' The further Shakespearean touch in this poem is of course unmistakable. The love of Romeo and Juliet was mutual, however star-crossed. The love in this poem is hopeless and solitary, 'star-defeated', for the speaker, before it even begins. The variant of Shakespeare's compound shows the speaker's, and the poet's, awareness of this.

Housman's poetry often produces a sudden vulnerability, which takes off the predictability of the way the poems themselves often work. 'Along the field as we come by' (*ASL*, xxvi), the aspen is whispering to the young man that he 'shall sleep with the clover clad' and 'his girl beside another lad'. Like many another, the poem is frank about enjoying its own sad tale, and its unillusioned acceptance of the way things go. But its true vulnerability comes out in the unexpected simplicity with which the speaker, like Hardy, 'notices' things: like the aspen itself, with 'its rainy-sounding silver leaves'. 'Rainy-sounding' has an enchanting rightness, simpler than any epithet even Hardy would use, and this simplicity takes over the almost facetiously conventional little plot of the poem, giving it the pathos of what seems a real event.

'The night is freezing fast' (*LP*, xx) is a particularly interesting case of what could be called Housman's reversed facetiousness:

> The night is freezing fast,
>   To-morrow comes December;
>   And winterfalls of old
>   Are with me from the past;
>   And chiefly I remember
>   How Dick would hate the cold.
>
> Fall, winter, fall; for he,
>   Prompt hand and headpiece clever,
>   Has woven a winter robe,
>   And made of earth and sea
>   His overcoat for ever,
>   And wears the turning globe.

I think most readers find the poem memorable, but at the same time a bit distasteful or glib. It passed the test of Housman's favour and was included in *Last Poems*, while another graceful piece with a similar diminuendo movement, 'I to my perils' (*MP*, vi) was left out. The latter may have struck the poet at some later date as too complacent, or self-gratified; but there is no knowing; 'The night is freezing fast', which occurs in Notebook D, may also be fairly late in time of composition. And it has attracted a good deal of critical attention. Cleanth Brooks and John Wain, contributors to Ricks's collection of essays, both single it out; the former finding it 'one of Housman's finest poems' and the latter both whimsical and over-artful, even the work of a poet whose poetry 'proves he was not a very intelligent man'.

A connoisseur of the metaphysical style, Brooks is impressed by the way the conceit of the poem is handled, and by the contrasting use of the commonplace word 'overcoat'. The conceit emphasises that 'the earth has not swallowed up Dick but that the dead man has wrapped the earth about himself'.

The man never at a loss has finally outwitted the cold, which he always used to hate. This at least is the way in which one might

imagine Dick's accounting for the situation. It is a gay piece of
schoolboy extravagance, and the jest, because it is characteristic of
the dead youth, actually renders the sense of grief not less but more
intense.*

Wain thinks the poem might well be a conscious or
unconscious imitation of Wordsworth's 'A slumber did my
spirit seal', and he finds that 'the whimsey of the diction'—the
archaic 'robe' with the facetious 'headpiece' and the commonplace 'overcoat'—contrasts with 'the truthful simplicity' of
Wordsworth's language, and goes with 'the silly suggestion
that it was clever of Dick to get into the earth to keep warm'.†
(Housman's detractors not infrequently accuse him of silliness.)

   Although both critics find sound technical reasons for the
conclusions they come to, our impression none the less may be
that theirs is an immediate human reaction, a response to a
personality and a tone. In the same way two critics might
differ sharply about things in Keats's poetry: one finding them
mawkish and distasteful, and another touching and true. It is
in the nature of a certain sort of romantic poetry not only to
provoke such opposite responses but to contain them—actually
to *need* them—in terms of a total effect. So it is with Housman,
or so it can be. It is, in a sense, a question of whether or not
you see the joke. 'The night is freezing fast' may be—and at
one and the same time—a clever poem, a touching poem, and
a silly poem. Certainly its readers seem to find it a memorable
one.

   The kind of balance implied here must often be precarious,
depending as it does on a tone, and the reader's response to
the complexity of tone. There seems no doubt that the poem
contradicts in some sort of way its own evident neat and
spruce pattern. Feeling breaks in, the kind of feeling that is
sharp contrast to the conceit about the overcoat, and yet a
part of it, for that conceit can be seen as a kind of excuse for
the sentimental. Cleanth Brooks himself feels there is 'not a
trace of sentimentality' in the poem, while observing that
Housman can at times fail disastrously in terms of tone and of

---

* Ricks (ed.), A. E. Housman: A Collection of Critical Essays.
† Ibid.

sentiment. It might rather be said that in some of his most
interesting poems failure and success, on these terms, can be
involved with each other. The form and manner of 'The night
is freezing fast' might be said to be designed to keep out what
is sentimental; but they could equally be designed to keep it
in—on their own terms.

One of the strengths of the poem, and one of the ways it
reaches out to human inadequacy, which finds solace in a
joke, is the open question of who is talking, and in what
context. ('A slumber did my spirit seal' is similarly open, in its
own more mysterious context.) And what Wordsworth in
another poem calls 'the impotence of grief' has its own
generalizing power inside Housman's lively, even perky,
stanzas. Whoever had the overcoat idea—and Brooks may be
right that it associates with the remembered personality of
Dick—the flippancy of the joke makes sadness more poignant.
The ground of loss does not reveal its depth, just as it does not
vouchsafe its relationship; and it is this uncertainty which
makes the poem continue to vibrate in its own way. A mother
or father could be grieving for Dick as a schoolboy, or as a
young man; a friend or a lover might be doing the same; a wife
might be grieving for her husband, remembering how she
mended his clothes and kept him warm. The poem about Lot
(*MP*, xxxv) hides a similar brief and undercover generalization
of sympathy, as if poet and reader were both Lot and Lot's
wife. The pathos of all loss, of any grief, is there in the
background, unable to make itself fanciful or dramatic. That
job is left to the poem, whose vibration about the nature of loss
strikes all the deeper for being passed over so lightly, and
having such lively substitutes found for it. The poem has all
the underlying pathos of a joke, even of a joke in the wrong
place.

CHAPTER 11

Hell Gate and Parnassus

Housman's pieces in the *Classical Review* or the *Journal of Philology* are always impressive, even to those who know little of the subject, and they are often very funny as well. It is hard to recall with a straight face his comments on the scholar who proposed to render hexameters in English with as many monosyllabic endings as possible, observing that 'if we do not like them at first we must get used to them.' Housman points out the drawbacks of such an attitude (one by no means uncommon, incidentally, among our practitioners of the contemporary arts) by proposing to take the same line in building houses. Why not use gingerbread as a building material, and if purchasers complained when they fell through the floor, or when the rain came in, just tell them they must get used to the way the thing was made?

The ideas about quantity advocated by W. J. Stone were not suited to our native stress and accent, and it is perverse to do a job with unsuitable materials when sound local ones exist. Thanking Robert Bridges for the poems of G. M. Hopkins, Housman remarked that 'Sprung Rhythm, as he calls it in his sober and sensible preface, is just as easy to write as other forms of verse', and natural to English; but it becomes unnatural when 'he does not make it audible', when 'he puts light syllables in the stress and heavy syllables in the slack, and has to be helped out with typographical signs explaining that things are to be understood as being what in fact they are not'.

Humour and swift good sense were always with him, where matters of poetry or metre were concerned. The earlier sallies—on finding the right meaning in Virgil's verses, or those of his brother Laurence—are the funniest, and the ones that go spontaneously to the heart of the matter. Later criticisms are more elaborate and more sardonic; and it was then that he took to storing shafts of wit for future use against erring commentators. Like other famous men he had a manner to keep up, his own sort of reputation to sustain; and like other famous men he both needed and disliked the task. He escaped when he could, particularly from interviewers. 'Tell him that some men are more interesting than their books but my book is more interesting than its man', he wrote to his publisher in 1921. '. . . Tell him anything.' Being the author of *A Shropshire Lad* was a burden; the need to maintain fastidious standards a still greater one. Politely declining the office of Public Orator at Cambridge, he remarked that friends who suggested it had no notion 'what a slow and barren mind I have, nor what a trouble composition is to me (in prose I mean: poetry is either easy or impossible)'. That was in 1920, and he did not enlarge on the question of whether he was still writing poetry.

In fact he was. He had heard from Moses Jackson in Canada, who was to die about the time *Last Poems* came out, when Housman was 63. *Last Poems*, in the course of preparation sometimes referred to by him as 'New Poems', was partly made up of things begun earlier or left at the idea stage. In a burst of activity some things may have come easily, some by the process he wryly referred to as 'impossible'. And 'Hell Gate' seems to have been one of these latter. It was finished in April 1922, becoming No. 31 in *Last Poems*, but it may have been begun a long time before, possibly in a different form. 'The piece I myself am most in doubt about is the longest', Housman wrote to his friend J. W. Mackail, 'and I fear that is not its worst fault.'

'About "Hell Gate" my troubles were, first, that the whole thing is on the edge of the absurd: if it does not topple over, that is well so far. Secondly, as you perceive, the texture of the diction, especially in the parts which I had to compose, is not what it should be, and I rather despair of mending it.' One cannot imagine Housman remarking that anything in *A Shropshire Lad* was on the edge of the absurd, or in danger of toppling over: if they were, that was, so to speak, nothing to do with him. The present attitude is much more deliberative, and goes with the emphasis on 'the parts which I had to compose'. The interest of 'Hell Gate', and why it tells us what it does about Housman as a poet, is that it is so much 'composed'. The texture of the diction seems intimately connected with the

happy outcome of the poem, happy in a sense that very
obviously recalls Adam and Eve, with the world all before
them, at the end of *Paradise Lost*. It may seem a little bizarre
that happiness and a fantasy composition should go with a
Miltonic model: later on in his letter to Mackail Housman
mentions 'the L'Allegro of my great exemplar'. So unlikely a
happy ending for Housman, in an escape from the power of
darkness and in a kind of wish-fulfilment, seen well-expressed
in a language he was not at ease in, and would have 'mended'
if he could.

Why was he not at ease? Perhaps because the story of the
poem was not to be taken seriously, a reverse of the spirit in
which Milton took the tale of Hell's revolt from Heaven. In
one sense, as we have seen, a poetry like Housman's takes
nothing quite seriously, but that is because it is about
naturally serious matters: love and grief and longing and
deprivation. But there might seem to be no way in which
Housman could be Housman when inventing a story about
sin and hell, and hell's master defied and shot by a mutinous
subject for the sake of his friend, the pair then making their
escape together in Boys' Own Paper style. The trouble about
wish-fulfilment fantasy is that one cannot easily make a joke of
it, the kind of joke about himself that Housman makes here:

> Twice a week the winter thorough
>   Here stood I to keep the goal:
> Football then was fighting sorrow
>   For the young man's soul.
>
> Now in Maytime to the wicket
>   Out I march with bat and pad:
> See the son of grief at cricket
>   Trying to be glad.
>
> Try I will; no harm in trying . . .
>   (*ASL*, xvii)

Young Housman as *homme sportif* is a real but thoroughly
ironized self-projection, an aspect of the wholehearted and
eager interest he took in the playing-field exploits of the two
Jackson brothers. 'Try I will; no harm in trying . . .' This is
the kind of wry wish-fulfilment his poetry understands.

It may be instructive to have a look at another of the *Last*

Poems, 'When the eye of day is shut' (LP, xxxiii), about which Housman also had a word for Mackail. Parts of it, one could say, also have the stamp of 'composition':

> When the eye of day is shut,
>   And the stars deny their beams,
> And about the forest hut
>   Blows the roaring wood of dreams,
>
> From deep clay, from desert rock,
>   From the sunk sands of the main,
> Come not at my door to knock,
>   Hearts that loved me not again.

Housman wrote to Mackail: 'I must confess I do not know what lines 3 and 4 mean'. He added that he thought 'forest hut', which he had written originally, might be better than 'hunter's hut', the form used in the manuscript he sent Mackail. It seems likely that the double negative came of itself, a negative that in emphasizing how little he wants to be visited also suggests both that he yearns to be, and that he knows the hearts did not love him, even if they return. In the depth of the poem it makes no difference if they loved him, for it is a vision of the lost: those whose loss makes them all the same and all indifferent now, whether they loved him once or not. The last verse emphasizes their dispersal still more deeply:

> In gross marl, in blowing dust,
>   In the drowned ooze of the sea,
> Where you would not, lie you must,
>   Lie you must, and not with me.

That they are so far gone, 'joined to the great sunk silences' as Isaac Rosenberg wrote in 1917 in his poem 'Dead Mans' Dump', is more forcibly expressed than the afterthought that goes with it. Like another of the *Last Poems*, 'In midnights of November' (*LP*, xix), the vibration of the poem is in its vision of the dead ('The leafless timber roars, | And the dead call the dying | And finger at the doors') rather than in the stock conclusion. That vision imposes its own meaning without the poem working it out.

But Housman could not have said about 'Hell Gate' that he did not know what it meant. The worst of that poem is that it

is grounded in literature as well as being a fantasy about life—
a life that never existed for Housman and could never have
existed, a life based on his dream of

> Soldiers of another corps
> And a sentry known before.

The fantasy of comradeship and a soldier's life also inspired *A
Shropshire Lad*, but there it was the real thing—Housman's
own real thing, seen with his own eyes—while 'Hell Gate' can
only use the eyesight of books. 'Literature', as he remarked in
the Swinburne essay, 'is neither a fruitful nor even an
appropriate subject for poetry'; and he adds the satirical dig
that Swinburne 'cannot watch a sunset at sea without
beginning to think about Beaumont and Fletcher'. Naturally
enough, he himself could hardly write about Satan and Hell
without invoking Milton. And it follows that although the
reader is very conscious of Housman's 'vibration' in the poem,
and can feel it himself, that vibration is detached from the
formal way the poem moves, works, keeps its footing.

The poet's concern lest the whole thing should 'topple over'
means that he concentrates on keeping the tone, and that
preservation can only make for an invulnerably spruce
pastiche. That adjective itself rebounds on him in 'Hell Gate',
with a lightness too conscious, almost deprecating, as the
flaming sentinel's 'spruce attire'. 'I think it is the right word',
he told Mackail, and helps, like ' "finery of fire", to keep the
piece from being too solemn.' That is altogether too sensible a
purpose, and a fatal precaution. It is not solemnity that
threatens the poem, but a conscious jauntiness (we remember
the reference to 'L'Allegro') which in this context seems
almost nervous in case the reader should be moved. Leaning
on its style the poem hastens the reader on to its effective
ending. 'Spruce' was indeed 'the right word', the more so
because Housman refers it to Milton's line about 'the spruce
and jocund spring'. 'The alternative to "spruce" is "brave" ',
Housman told his friend, 'which I like less, partly because it
has the same vowel sound as "failed" in the next line. What do
you think?'

Such a request seems to show that the poet himself thought
the poem 'on the edge of the absurd' in a perfectly jolly and

acceptable way, rather like a nonsense poem which could be read out and laughed about in public without disturbing the author's privacy or his *amour propre*. Or was Housman kidding on the level again? The poem might belong to that class which Ricks remarks on, where the movement and demeanour of the verse—as in 'I to my perils | Of cheat and charmer'—is deliberately in contrast with the sobriety or intensity of its subject. But the objection here is that 'Hell Gate' does in fact seem all of a piece, in tone and treatment, a sprucely literary affair throughout. There is no instability about it, no intrusion of an emotional vibration into a formal pattern, as there is in so many poems; and indeed in another of the *Last Poems*, 'When I would muse in Boyhood' (*LP*, xxxii):

> I sought them far and found them,
>   The sure, the straight, the brave,
> The hearts I lost my own to,
>   The souls I could not save.

'Brave' has its other sense here: not at all the sense of 'brave attire'.

'Hell Gate' may have suited Housman's intention to make *Last Poems* a more-or-less benevolent farewell, a gesture of unbending at parting analogous to those genialities he would proffer later in 'The Name and Nature of Poetry'. Disclosure itself might now be read as a form of dismissal, of literariness and leisure, even though the fact remains that the poem *is* a kind of undercover job, a confidence concealed in the open by its tone and provenance, and by the way the author is prepared to discuss its technical shortcomings. Who is the guard doomed to eternal sentry-go on the battlements of hell if not Housman himself—Alfred Edward—acting out a tongue-in-cheek fantasy of being not just an army man but one of the legion of the damned, 'Weaponed and accoutred well | From the arsenals of hell?'

> Ever darker hell on high
> Reared its strength upon the sky,
> And our footfall on the track
> Fetched the daunting echo back.
> But the soldier pacing still
> The insuperable sill,

> Nursing his tormented pride,
> Turned his head to neither side,
> Sunk into himself apart
> And the hell-fire of his heart.

Being 'sunk into himself apart', and 'nursing his tormented pride' were states with which the poet was familiar; but somehow this personification misses being a sardonic joke at his own expense, just as it misses communicating a moving emotional vibration. The whole thing is too easy, and too superficially 'thrilling'. Housman, like Milton or Browning, knows how to present the properties of a good yarn. 'Daunting' is good, and the idea of the perilous voyage is as exciting as that of the 'wary fiend' in *Paradise Lost*, or Childe Roland's to the Dark Tower. An inner and private hell is real, as the poet well knew, but the poetic one is made up, and not in the sense in which a Milton or Dante took it for granted that the hells they described had somewhere a true existence.

Indeed 'Hell Gate' has much in common with a poetic ideal of Housman's favourite critic, Matthew Arnold. Arnold had instructed modern culture not to attach imagination to the *fact*—the fact of damnation or resurrection or atonement—but to the *idea* of those things, which could not fail it. Such an idea is deliberately and inescapably literary; and in its own way 'Hell Gate' is doing what Arnold had done in 'Mycerinus' or 'Sohrab and Rustum', giving an inward and personal slant to a legendary tale. 'Hell Gate' is long by Housman's standards, but does the job with a brevity very different from Arnold's leisurely style. Housman had his own hell, of course, but he did not believe that the wages of sin are death, as the narrator reflects while travelling towards hell's gate with his 'dark conductor':

> Many things I thought of then,
> Battle, and the loves of men,
> Cities entered, oceans crossed,
> Knowledge gained and virtue lost,
> Cureless folly done and said . . .

These are a scholar's fantasies, like his dreams of the military life and 'a field afar'. So is the prostitute-portress Sin, who ogles the soldierly narrator. (' "Met again, my lass," said I').

Nothing wrong with fantasy; but this one, like Arnold's, has more of the study in it than the private world. And its strangest connection is with an author and a poem for which Housman had the strongest attachment, Horace and his ode, 'Diffugere Nives'. Housman's translation of it was first published in *The Quarto* in 1897, and included by his brother in *More Poems* (*MP*, v). A lady who attended his lectures at Trinity College in May 1914 has left a memory of him on one occasion 'reading the ode aloud with deep emotion, first in Latin and then in an English translation of his own', and leaving the room with the comment that he considered it 'the most beautiful poem in ancient literature'. When he gave this judgement, 'almost like a man betraying a secret', Housman had possibly already metamorphosed a reference in the ode into the story that was to become 'Hell Gate'. In the legend Theseus is rescued by Hercules from hell, but has to leave his old comrade there for ever.

> Night holds Hippolytus the pure of stain,
>   Diana steads him nothing, he must stay;
> And Theseus leaves Pirithoüs in the chain
>   The love of comrades cannot take away.

The tone of Housman's translation could not be more different from that of 'Hell Gate', which has been transformed into an adventure story with a happy ending. The sentry who mutinied and turned his musket on the master of hell ('But across the entry barred | Straddled the revolted guard'), the sentry who paced

> Trim and burning, to and fro,
> One for women to admire
> In his finery of fire

was not only 'sunk into himself apart | And the hell-fire of his heart', but cured this condition at one stroke by shooting the devil and rescuing the friend he had brought down to hell:

> Silent, nothing found to say,
> We began the backward way;
> And the ebbing lustre died
> From the soldier at my side,
> As in all his spruce attire

> Failed the everlasting fire.
> Midmost of the homeward track
> Once we listened and looked back;
> But the city, dusk and mute,
> Slept, and there was no pursuit.

The sentry is 'Ned'—Alfred Edward Housman—indulging like Walter Mitty in a dream of glory and saving the situation with one decisive stroke. And it is himself he saves: his friend the narrator does nothing, is a mere passive spectator; but he too is saved by the sentry's action, and was himself the cause of it.

The poem reverses not only the tenor of everything else Housman had written, but that of his own favourite Latin poem. The love of comrades *can* take away the chain, at least in the world of poetry and the imagination. But only at the cost of the sardonic poet himself not believing it, and not expecting his readers to do so. Don't shoot yourself; shoot the boss, and all your troubles will be over. Yet this is not humour, in Housman's usual sense, because it is at once too visible and too 'dressed up' in the fancy-dress of poetic form. The invisible tension in the relation of poet and reader has given way to a relaxed understanding, secret intimacy to open connivance.

Housman was deeply moved by the suicide of the Woolwich cadet in 1895, and by the letter he left for the coroner. 'There is only one thing in the world which would make me thoroughly happy; that one thing I have no earthly hope of obtaining.' The poem he wrote then, 'Shot? so quick, so clean an ending?' (*ASL*, xliv), is full of emotion and excitement, vibrating with a sympathy which its form keeps tightly under control:

> Oh soon, and better so than later
>   After long disgrace and scorn,
> You shot dead the household traitor,
>   The soul that should not have been born.

By shooting himself the cadet achieved for the poet what was later transformed into a romantic tale, and in the admirable movement of the early poem there is a current of real gratitude:

> Now to your grave shall friend and stranger
>   With ruth and some with envy come:
> Undishonoured, clear of danger,
>   Clear of guilt, pass hence and home.
>
> Turn safe to rest, no dreams, no waking;
>   And here, man, here's the wreath I've made:
> 'Tis not a gift that's worth the taking,
>   But wear it and it will not fade.

'Hell Gate' does show what a wide variety of effects could be achieved by Housman, and what good use he could make of other kinds of literature, as well as his own personal feeling. He never 'takes a header into literature', as Larkin said that the urbane manner of the later Auden tended to do, but at any stage of his career as a poet he could walk about on Parnassus and use whatever he found. Rather like Wallace Stevens's 'An Ordinary Evening in Newhaven', which uses Edward Lear's Corsican journals, or Eliot's more stylized use of quotation in *The Waste Land*, 'Hell Gate' spins its own quest-meditation out of a variety of sources. And Housman at any period can make good use of other things than poems. 'The Welsh Marches' (*ASL*, xxviii), is superb as a terse romance on history and geography:

> High the vanes of Shrewsbury gleam
> Islanded in Severn stream;
> The bridges from the steepled crest
> Cross the water east and west.
>
> The flag of morn in conqueror's state
> Enters at the English gate:
> The vanquished eve, as night prevails,
> Bleeds upon the road to Wales.

Never mind that the directions come out of the county guide, as some of Auden's in his early poems do. In both cases the authority and urgency of the poetry takes over the place, giving it new and pointed significance. Shrewsbury bridges, unlike Hell Gate, have nothing received or Parnassian about them; and the poet hardly needs to point the moral that his heart, like the marches, is the scene of age-old war, oppression, hatred between sex and race.

An echo of Sappho is not Parnassian either. 'The weeping

Pleiads wester' (*MP* x) hides its own story in the four inner
lines of an eight-line poem which invokes its original:

> From bourn to bourn of midnight
> > Far sighs the rainy breeze:
> It sighs from a lost country
> > To a land I have not known . . .

The lost land of childhood, and unknown India, come
together in the poem's aloneness, visited only by the night
wind and the stars known to the Greek female poet of the
ancient world. Sappho, unlike Satan, is a figure in whom the
poem believes, and with whom it identifies. But Housman can
make the error of using astronomy, the subject of his Latin
poet Manilius, in a way in which ingenuity removes pathos.
'Astronomy' (*LP*, xvii) must have been written after his
youngest brother, a regular in the army, was killed in the Boer
War:

> For pay and medals, name and rank,
> > Things that he has not found,
> He hove the Cross to heaven and sank
> > The pole-star underground.

> And now he does not even see
> > Signs of the nadir roll
> At night over the ground where he
> > Is buried with the pole.

The attention we must give to stellar matters runs out of series
with sorrow for the dead. Ingenuity of stars and crosses
clutters the poem's brief movement; and it is rather too
pointed a double meaning that Sergeant Housman, who
performed these feats for military advancement, should be
seen as heaving the cross high, as if it were a heavy piece of
equipment. Such loaded emphases are as out of place here as
they are successful and appropriate in other celestial contexts,
like 'Revolution' (*LP*, xxxvi), or 'Reveille' (*ASL*, iv). In
'Drummer Hodge', also written at the time of Boer War,
Hardy used the point about stars in a moving and simpler
form.

 If 'Hell Gate' has any inner life it is a sort of academic one,
as if Housman was making, in his public style, one of the jokes

shared among scholars. Satan, guiding his new recruit down
to hell, praises his quick understanding of its topographical
layout, as a beginner might be praised for his reading of
manuscript by a senior colleague:

> . . . my dark conductor broke
> Silence at my side and spoke,
> Saying, 'You conjecture well:
> Yonder is the gate of hell.'

Satan is more easygoing than his recruit, who rarely allowed a
conjecture to pass uncriticized; but the arrangements in hell
might strike us as more like those of a senior common room,
even though the damned 'Ned' is there assigned his sentry-
duty, 'sunk into himself apart'. Housman, after all, did not
always take his own troubles very seriously. There seem to be
many moments in *Last Poems* when he enjoys being gloomy,
even seeming to enjoy—and sardonically, amid the bland
glow of pessimism—the contrast they make with some of the
poems in *A Shropshire Lad*—'From far, from eve and morning'
or 'Into my heart an air that kills'. In one of his last letters he
describes himself as 'a Cyrenaic . . . hedonist', one who
regards 'the pleasure of the moment as the only possible
motive of action'; and the pleasure of the moment, as he
mellowed into age, was often too ostensibly a gloomy one.

  In 'The chestnut casts his flambeaux' (*LP*, ix) or the brief
poem that follows it, 'Could man be drunk for ever' (LP, x),
the tone seems selected too deliberately to contrast with the
state of man which the words evoke. Indeed it is in the former
poem that what Housman wrote to Mackail about 'Hell
Gate'—'the whole thing is on the edge of the absurd'—is in
danger of being true. Housman's dispassionate poems are
seldom quite detached enough to seem dramatized, although
'There's one spoilt spring to scant our mortal lot' seems
admirably to convey the over-careful articulation caused by
excess of ale. So does the slight hiccup at the opening of the
fifth verse:

> It is in truth iniquity on high
>   To cheat our sentenced souls of aught they crave,
> And mar the merriment as you and I
>   Fare on our long fool's-errand to the grave.
> Iniquity it is; but pass the can.

Acoustically the thing is almost too well set up. Young readers (this was perhaps the point and the intention) can and do remember it with admiration and enjoyment. But there can be something faintly uneasy about the older Housman's tone and intentions, as if he were taking too much, and too private, pleasure in the way the thing was working. Is it always working as well for us?

One such poem seems very Delphic indeed, which is why it may have remained unpublished in Housman's lifetime. 'Far known to sea and shore' (*MP*, xliv) commemorates the fall and the rebuilding of the campanile at Venice, completed not long before the First World War:

> Far known to sea and shore,
>   Foursquare and founded well,
> A thousand years it bore
>   And then the belfry fell.
> The steersman of Triest
>   Looked where his mark should be,
> But empty was the west
>   And Venice under sea.*

'On surer foot than first' the belfry is rebuilt; and the toll of its bell at evening again 'burdens far away | The green and sanguine shoals'.

> It looks to north and south,
>   It looks to east and west;
> It guides to Lido mouth
>   The steersman of Triest.
> Andrea, fare you well;
>   Venice, farewell to thee.
> The tower that stood and fell
>   Is not rebuilt in me.

Andrea could be a phantom friend, like Dick, or like the phantom other self, the military comrade of 'Hell Gate'. In fact he was a real person, a gondolier whom Housman employed on his visits to Venice. In one sense the poem is light, regretful, gracefully contrasting the rebuilding of the campanile and the continuity of Venetian life with the termination of the poet's visits. But there is also a deeper

* The stanza arrangement is that made by Housman's brother for *More Poems*.

cadence of regret, the notion of an abandonment. Housman must have been well aware of the significance of the image with which he ends the poem. Whether Andrea the gondolier would have been aware of it is another question, for their relations were probably wholly decorous. But the eye and the imagination knows no decorum, and nor does legendary and literary Venice. Who but Housman could have combined the vibrations in one poem, each seemingly unaware of the other? The first is beautifully conventional: the Byronic farewell to roving; the exile's lament of Burns transposed into this southern setting. The second is in a sudden whiff of the louche, the bad taste that lurks invisibly, though perhaps deliberately, at the climax of the final stanza. And the verses too are dense with local allusion, bred as much by the place as by the authors who wrote about it—Browning and Shakespeare, Byron and Baron Corvo.

The poem seems both fresh and tarnished, for Housman's accurate eye had observed from campanile or gondola the shallows of the lagoon—'the green and sanguine shoals'—and memorializes their hues as Macbeth had done; while the music of the verse, like Browning's toccata of Galluppi, heralds the end of the sensualities of living, 'at to-fall of the day'. Not the finality of love but the transitoriness of sexual enjoyment makes a tone appropriately both stoical and epicurean. More subtle than the physical symbolism of the tower is the concluding cadence in which the poet seems to deprecate an application of the poem's subject to himself. The last word is self-contradictory: not rebuilt in me, but rebuilt in the poem for the reader. The poem is a device not so much to rebuild a personal experience as to make it seem both personal and compelling to a later reader. Its final effect is that reliable old favourite the sense of loss, changed into an experience of discovery: 'sorrow that is not sorrow, but delight'.

Housman was never more at home on Parnassus than in this Venice poem. It is the prime example of Larkin's 'verbal device' to reproduce emotion (the arch romantic effect) 'in anyone who cares to read it, anywhere, any time'. But when either poet takes someone else's private episode as a poem's subject the result is usually inert, although as competent as anyone would expect. Larkin's poem 'Deceptions', on the ruined girl from the pages of Mayhew, has something not quite right about it; it seems almost an 'offering' poem, like his little one for the newly born Sally Amis, 'Born Yesterday'. Housman has some comparable offerings. Moses Jackson returned from India to be married in 1889, and although Housman did not attend his wedding or hear of it at the time, he composed an 'Epithalamium' (*LP*, xxiv). How long after the event is not certain, but it seems likely the poem was not finally completed until 1922, the year when Housman heard of Jackson's illness, and assembled *Last Poems* for publication just before his death. 'Epithalamium', with its inevitably happy ending, has some of the characteristics of 'Hell Gate', using the same Miltonic style and metre with the same kind of accomplishment:

> Safe you sleep on guarded ground,
> And in silent circle round
> The thoughts of friends keep watch and ward,
> Harnessed angels, hand on sword.

Although she had been married before, young Mrs Jackson might well have felt a little intimidated by the scenario of her new husband's friends, armed and watchful round the bed, having reluctantly yielded him to her embraces. Hymen, Urania's son, is here 'both' to join and part; the bridegroom to be yielded by friend and comrade, 'To her that hardly loves you more'.

Housman could not write at his best to order, however willingly he might himself have given the order, and the results usually have something Parnassian about them in the sense in which Hopkins used the term: a falling back upon writing the 'kind' of poetry that the poet writes; but poetry from which his true individuality (and in Housman's case his true humour) must needs be absent. Housman detected the process in Swinburne, as he would have diagnosed it in Wordsworth, or in Wallace Stevens. Housman in the grip of the poetry that was 'easy', that came to him out of the air, never seems to practise self-imitation, voluntary or involuntary; but the poems that were more laboriously produced are a different matter. This is shown by one of the best-documented, (Her strong enchantments failing' (*LP*, iii), which was published as 'The Conflict' in the magazine of King Edward's

School, Bath, where Housman's nephew had been a pupil. The poem was originally set up as no. 43 in *A Shropshire Lad*, and had been removed by Housman in page proof. Why? Perhaps because he sensed it was too hortatory, as some of the least successful poems in *A Shropshire Lad* are, and not personal enough. According to Laurence Housman, he sent the poem to his nephew soon after the outbreak of the First World War, in which the young man was later killed. Whether or not it had a bracing effect we cannot be sure, but the nephew copied it out and left it with his mother, Housman's sister.

Some years later Housman explained in a letter that 'the queen of air and darkness' who figures in the poem came 'from a line of Coventry Patmore's—'the powers of darkness and the air', and that this in its turn was a reference to 'the prince of the power of the air' in Ephesians 2:2. 'And the meaning is evil', remarks Housman. If so, it was evil very much in the sense in which Satan and hell represent their originals in 'Hell Gate'. And such evil can be overcome at a blow: putting the pistol to your head, shooting Satan, cutting the throat of the queen of air and darkness. These are the day-dream acts of a romantic poetry, going through its own motions, very different from that intensity of the personal and the individual found in *A Shropshire Lad* or—and in a different fashion—in the poem on Venice and its campanile. Communal day-dream, public exhortation, deprive Housman of his unique self.

The melodrama of the queen of air and darkness deprives its poem of personal feeling, in much the same manner that the public day-dream of 'Hell Gate' does. But sometimes a poem that bears all the marks of composition, instead of those characteristic inspirations that came into the poet's head, can none the less display all the immediacy and sureness of his best work. A good example is 'Easter Hymn' (*MP*, i) unpublished by Housman but probably retouched and revised over the years. In a sense its topic is one that much exercised thoughtful Victorians, and forms the basis of such now-forgotten works as Samuel Butler's *The Fair Haven*. The poet who went to church, and even took communion in order not to seem odd or disobliging to old friends, might not have wished a 'Hymn' which calmly propounds such a very divisive issue to appear in his lifetime.

If, in that Syrian garden, ages slain,
You sleep, and know not you are dead in vain,
Nor even in dreams behold how dark and bright
Ascends in smoke and fire by day and night
The hate you died to quench and could but fan,
Sleep well and see no morning, son of man.

But if, the grave rent and the stone rolled by,
At the right hand of majesty on high
You sit, and sitting so remember yet
Your tears, your agony and bloody sweat,
Your cross and passion and the life you gave,
Bow hither out of heaven and see and save.

Poetry can square the circle, or at least present an alternative
where choice is not the point. It could be a hymn sung in
church, like the one Housman composed for his own funeral: a
choir might anthem it without the congregation being aware
that it was in any way unusual. Orthodoxy is not in the habit
of offering an alternative to the worshipper; but there are ways
of doing it, as Housman's admired Matthew Arnold was well
aware. Housman's position is implicit in a line from Larkin's
poem 'Church Going', also a title without irony. 'And what
remains when disbelief has gone' indicates our lack of need for
either the one state or the other, implied already in Housman's
mellifluous alternative. If belief goes, then disbelief goes too,
sooner or later. What remains may be nebulous, but
consciousness likes it, even needs it. Many hymns have
inadvertently turned the Christian legend into mild words of
comfort and communion: Housman's words are not mild, for
all their air of calm. The horror of the crucifixion, of man's
hatred for man, seem felt the more deeply in the poem the less
important it is to relate them to an orthodox faith and belief.

Christopher Ricks writes that 'Easter Hymn' does, in its
way, make a prayer to Christ: 'Bow hither out of heaven and
see and save.' But how? 'In the only real way', says Ricks, 'by
granting oblivion, the gift of eternal death, such as Christ
himself must now, or would now, yearn for.' But the hymn
does not quite say that: it says something much simpler. If
Christ were really there, eternal and immortal, he could
redeem us through his resurrection, as he himself promised.
When disbelief has gone, as it probably had with Housman,

there is no point in our objecting to the idea of such a salvation. Salvation, or oblivion, are two separate human hopes and ideals, both of which can none the less offer us the same kind of comfort. And both do so, in their own way, in the poem.

'Easter Hymn' may move us not only with the mastery of its calmly articulated syntax but by offering an alternative which does not require choice, certainly not a 'spiritual' choice. It operates rather as Housman thought Blake's 'mystical' poetry did, solely through the operation of the poetical: which of course includes our knowledge of the story, and our sense of the pity in it. The movement of the poem's thoughts, as in 'Lycidas', 'dally with fale surmise', and for the same reason: 'so as to impose a little ease.' Milton, speculating on the whereabouts of his drowned young friend, can put the matter as he does because he can use mythology quite separately from religious truth, and in contrast to it. But in a post-Arnold religious context the idea is everything; Housman is doing the same thing as Wilfred Owen does in his moving poem 'Asleep', on the fate of a dead soldier:

> Whether his deeper sleep lie shaded by the shaking
> Of great wings, and the thoughts that hung the stars:
> High-pillowed on calm pillows of God's making
> Above these clouds, these pains, these sleets of lead,
> And these winds' scimitars;
> —Or whether yet his thin and sodden head
> Confuses more and more with the low mould,
> His hair being one with the grey grass
> And finished fields of autumns that are old . . .
> Who knows? Who hopes? Who troubles?—let it pass!

Owen's rhetoric, some of it not of a standard that would pass Housman's scrutiny, throws us at once into the pity of the situation, rather than into a consideration of life after death, a matter, incidentally, which the casualties of war had thrust into prominence: the spiritualists were having a field-day transmitting reassuring messages from the 'other side'. In Owen's words the image of a celestial sleep on God's pillow blends into that of a corpse drawn indistinguishably into the sodden earth. As with Housman's Hymn, both possibilities are sustained movingly within the poetic trope. The horror of

Celan's 'Engführung' was also reconciled with its comfort by an injunction not to read, not even to look: an injunction which works to ensure the act of remembering, of the words of the poem as memorable speech.

It is a poetry that fills the gap when disbelief has gone, but when memory and desire attend consciousness until the moment of extinction.

> We now to peace and darkness
> And earth and thee restore
> Thy creature that thou madest
> And wilt cast forth no more.

Housman's funeral hymn would hardly have raised an eyebrow in Trinity College chapel, although Ricks feels he might have savoured the service in anticipation. Its impact depends on an air of total decorum, together with what seems an inescapable punch of meaning: and yet the decorum of the lines contrives to join up with the meaning, so that the hope of eternal life and the certainty of oblivion meet together in sardonic accord.

More Poems—the ones which Housman rejected as not up to his standards or perhaps had only a private liking for, contains several of these terse little Stanley-and-Livingstone encounters between neighbourly incompatibilities of meaning. And the final little sheaf of *Additional Poems* has a particularly notable one:

> When the bells justle in the tower
> The hollow night amid,
> Then on my tongue the taste is sour
> Of all I ever did.
>
> (*AP*, ix)

There seems to be an oral tradition that Housman made this up in a dream, although in later life he could not recall having done so. Laurence Housman noted that verse sometimes came to his brother in dreams, which seems the more likely considering how they came to him at restful moments in waking life. If the poem really arrived in a dream it was certainly worked on in the poet's waking hours, for the manuscript contains a number of uncancelled variants, including a third line which reads 'Then to my heart the thought is sour'. The options in Housman's manuscripts usually remain open, as they do in this case; but Christopher Ricks has remarked on the felicity of the word 'tongue', no doubt suggested by the rhyme-word 'sour', but then joining itself, in what is indeed a *curiosa felicitas*, to bells, which not only have tongues but the metallic taste of brass. Shakespeare, Milton, and Keats ran trains along similar lines of association. But in Housman's case the train is apt to reverse itself invisibly, for 'all I ever did' is also present as richness and pleasure in the heavy stroke of the short verse. The dream-odd word 'justle' conveys not the sound but the movement of bells, and thus other movements: the dance of sense and conscious-ness, the rustle of clothing; richness both regarded in the verse and shunned in its isolation.

Whatever else he is doing Housman needs to be forceful, and his clarities need to startle us, or to set up a counter-vibration. When he is too Parnassian, and gets in his own groove of choice diction and suave exposition, the result can have a predictability of its own. Cleanth Brooks complained of a line in 'Bredon Hill' (*ASL*, xxi).

> They tolled the one bell only,
>   Groom there was none to see,
> The mourners followed after,
>   And so to church went she,
>   And would not wait for me.

Housman had great trouble with that verse, and Brooks felt that the third line showed he never got it quite right. Why have mourners to show the reader what had happened? As Housman said to his brother, it is a question of how and when that 'man of sorrows' is to find out what it is all about; and he helps the reader with great and inconspicuous skill, often by the intuitional method he so much admired in Blake. Brooks may be right that the mourners need not have featured in that famous poem, yet the poem demonstrates Housman's power of dramatic concentration, in ballad style, while exercising an effective invisible control. 'Fancy's Knell', placed to conclude *Last Poems*, shows the same skill in more graceful, Parnassian form, Housman's touch being specially evident in the counter-

point between the flute that plays through the poem, and the
silence of the dancers:

> The girl would lift her glances
> To his, and both be mute . . .

The most Parnassian of *Last Poems* (*LP*, xl) precedes it, and in
its completed form can be dated with fair certainty to April
1922. Its approach is smooth, its beauty full of a possibly
rather feline sophistication.

> Tell me not here, it needs not saying,
> What tune the enchantress plays
> In aftermaths of soft September
> Or under blanching mays,
> For she and I were long acquainted
> And I knew all her ways.

The enchantress is already at work, turning the late-mown
grass into what sounds like a girl's name, as if soft September
and May, seductresses identified with their flowering trees
and their autumn fields, were attendant upon her own more-
elusive charms.

> On russet floors, by waters idle,
> The pine lets fall its cone;
> The cuckoo shouts all day at nothing
> In leafy dells alone;
> And traveller's joy beguiles in autumn
> Hearts that have lost their own.
>
> On acres of the seeded grasses
> The changing burnish heaves;
> Or marshalled under moons of harvest
> Stand still all night the sheaves;
> Or beeches strip in storms for winter
> And stain the wind with leaves.
>
> Possess, as I possessed a season,
> The countries I resign,
> Where over elmy plains the highway
> Would mount the hills and shine,
> And full of shade the pillared forest
> Would murmur and be mine.
>
> For nature, heartless, witless nature,
> Will neither care nor know

> What stranger's feet may find the meadow
>   And trespass there and go,
> Nor ask amid the dews of morning
>   If they are mine or no.

This almost literally enchanting poem might seem to depend upon the vibration set up in the reader's consciousness by the emotion felt by the poet at the thought that nature, who is stupid as well as unfeeling, used to seduce him with her beauties, but is now faithless, no longer giving herself to him but to some stranger who makes free with her charms in the poet's old haunts. The poet's disillusionment seems to include a grim realization of just how fickle nature's charms really are; but not to suggest that he can no longer feel them in the poignant way Wordsworth expresses in the 'Immortality Ode' his sense that 'The things that I have seen I now can see no more'. It is not the poet's fault but nature's, the deceiving enchantress, whom the poet willingly resigns to some successor. The trouble is that by the time he has enjoyed and considered the poem the reader does not really believe all this. Even as he reads the poem it becomes more and more clear—enchantingly clear—that the pillared forest and the pine-cone, the cuckoo and traveller's joy, are there for their own sake, and for this finely haunting evocation of them. The enchantress is not like the Siren who tempted Ulysses with unexpectedly domestic delights, setting up the unexpected feeling which vibrates in Daniel's poem.

Perhaps the poet is as responsive as ever to nature, and is only making believe to feel disillusioned with her? He is, in a sense, teasing her, affecting to find her a jilt, not taking his own fancy all that seriously, not wanting—or expecting—the reader to do so either. Certainly the idea in the poem has been taken seriously by critics, including William Empson, who praised it, but thought the point made one of the silliest and most perverse imaginable.* This is to take it in a different spirit from what Housman himself would have called 'non-sense'—asking for one's kisses back again; or asking not to be asked where Jove bestows, when June is past, the fading rose. Empson, of course, pays Housman the thoroughly deserved

---

* *British Journal of Aesthetics* 2 (1962), 40–1. See also Christoper Ricks, *The Force of Poetry*, 177.

compliment, based on the unnerving good sense of most of his poems, of rejoining that this one should be sensible too. Ricks respects Empson, but maintains that the poem is indeed sensible, and forceful, because the enchantress is seen throughout in terms of a consistent and down-to-earth sexual symbolism ('I knew all her ways . . .', 'Would murmur and be mine'), and that the poem plays this off against that true sense of the sadness of impersonal nature of which the poet was always well aware ('The tears of morning | That weeps, but not for thee').

The success of the poem, in short, should come from a properly vigorous use of the Pathetic Fallacy, combined with a clear-eyed sense, on the poet's part, of the kind of nonsense the Fallacy must represent. And yet I remember, when first reading the poem, that though it pleased me very much there seemed something artificial about it: artificial in the sense that the beauty of the words describing the natural objects left those objects seeming unnatural. Those so-much chosen words—'elmy', 'pillared', 'burnish'—increased the sense of a country not in the mind—the blue remembered hills—or seen as part of living experience ('When smoke stood up from Ludlow, | And must blew off from Teme'), but as a museum for verbal exhibits, even that of the enchanting pine-cone, and the russet floor it falls on.

Housman here is not in the grip of his subject. There is no true inner feeling, for which he needs to find the poetic correlative. There are many ways, in many of his poems, where this drawback is overcome or loses meaning; but here the very success, the admirable pretension of the poem, makes it relevant. 'Bring, in this timeless grave to throw' (*ASL*, xlvi) for instance, is not an especially good poem, but it is moving, because the accuracy of the point made goes with the emotion that needed to make it. The poet imagines, for this 'timeless grove', no timeless memorial garland, no cypress, yew, rosemary, and no leafless bough that will bud in spring, but only an 'awn' or 'haulm' from the Christmas field which has a green stalk not be renewed, 'Or shrivelled flax, whose flower is blue | A single season, never two'.

> —Oh, bring from hill and stream and plain
> Whatever will not flower again,

> To give him comfort; he and those
> Shall bide eternal bedfellows.

The botanical point has nothing fussy about it; and the clumsy, homely 'awn' and 'haulm', signifying the weed-growth in a harvest field, perishing altogether before the coming spring, join the dead man with peculiar intensity in the poem's vision. 'Tell me not here' (*LP*, xl), seems to need its own kind of poignancy but does not find it; being left with the choice glimpses of natural beauty which leads on to a conclusion that is felt, certainly; but felt and worked out in the head rather than the heart.

There is an odd possible reason for this. In the preface to his edition of the fifth book of Manilius's *Astronomicon*, published in 1930, Housman quoted a poem by Walter de la Mare:

The following stanza of Mr de la Mare's 'Fare Well', first met my eyes, thus printed, in a newspaper review.

> Oh, when this my dust surrenders
> Hand, foot, lip, to dust again,
> May these loved and loving faces
>   Please other men!
> May the rustling harvest hedgerow
> Still the Traveller's Joy entwine,
> And as happy children gather
>   Posies once mine.

I knew in a moment that Mr de la Mare had not written *rustling*, and in another moment I had found the true word. But if the book of poems had perished and the verse survived only in the review, who would have believed me rather than the compositor? The bulk of the reading public would have been perfectly content with *rustling*, nay they would sincerely have preferred it to the epithet which the poet chose. If I had been so ill-advised as to publish my emendation, I should have been told that *rustling* was exquisitely apt and poetical, because hedgerows do rustle, especially in autumn, when the leaves are dry, and when straws and ears from the passing harvest-wain (to which 'harvest' is so plain an allusion that only a pedant like me could miss it) are hanging caught in the twigs; and I should have been recommended to quit my dusty (or musty) books and make a belated acquaintance with the sights and sounds of the English countryside.

Never one to leave well alone in this sort of context, Housman could not resist adding a final sentence. 'And the only possible answer could have been *ugh*!' Part of the effect, which we certainly do not grudge him, is that he does not bother to tell us what he knew the right word to be. To make sure we have to go to the text of Walter de la Mare's poems, where we find applied to the harvest hedgerow the adjective 'rusting'. More than that, we find a very beautiful poem, probably already familiar to us from the anthologies, very different in spirit from Housman's 'Tell me not here', but subtly related to it.

> Fare Well
> When I lie where shades of darkness
> Shall no more assail mine eyes,
> Nor the rain make lamentation
>   When the wind sighs;
> How will fare the world whose wonder
> Was the very proof of me?
> Memory fades, must the remembered
>   Perishing be?
>
> Oh, when this my dust surrenders
> Hand, foot, lip, to dust again,
> May these loved and loving faces
>   Please other men!
> May the rusting harvest hedgerow
> Still the Traveller's Joy entwine,
> And as happy children gather
>   Posies once mine.
>
> Look thy last on all things lovely
> Every hour. Let no night
> Seal thy sense in deathly slumber
>   Till to delight
> Thou have paid thy utmost blessing;
> Since that all things thou wouldst praise
> Beauty took from those who loved them
>   In other days.

'Fare Well' first appeared in Walter de la Mare's *Collected Poems* in 1920, and Housman no doubt read the review soon after, at a time when he was composing or completing his own selection for *Last Poems*, which appeared in 1922. F. W. Bateson thought that the reference to 'traveller's joy' (lower-case in Housman's poem) might have been borrowed from de

la Mare. I would speculate further that 'Tell me not here'
might well be, in some sense, an 'answer' to 'Fare Well'.

If so, it would be the only time Housman recognized the
existence, in his own poetry, of a fellow and contemporary
poet. As we have seen, he wrote to his publisher, Grant
Richards, in 1928, that to include him in an anthology of the
Nineties would be 'technically correct' but 'essentially in-
appropriate'. 'I hoed and trenched and weeded | And took the
flowers to fair', the concluding poem in *A Shropshire Lad*,
stylizes Housman's own feeling of isolation as a poet in his
time. 'The hue' of his verse 'was not the wear' then, though it
might catch the eye of a luckless lad when he was dead and
gone. Apart from good-natured remarks about his brother
Laurence's poetry, Housman seems to have felt little but mild
contempt for the verse of his contemporaries, not excluding de
la Mare's. The idea of being anthologized with him or with
W. E. Henley did not please; and although he wrote a letter
appreciating one of his poems to John Drinkwater, who had
been accused in a *Times* review of imitating him, it is clear that
he thought little of him as a poet. What Dr Johnson called 'the
mutual civilities of authors' must have seemed particularly
risible to Housman, but he observed them with punctilious
relish, sending Drinkwater a signed copy of *Last Poems* after
receiving the other poet's latest volume. (A few years later
Drinkwater invited himself to tea, and was politely requested
to come at four, because Housman wished to hear Paul Valéry
lecture on 'Poetic Inspiration' at five o'clock.) At an earlier
date Housman also expressed what seems genuine admiration
for some of John Davidson's poetry, and in 1922 he wrote to
Gilbert Murray that he had 'been admiring Blunden for some
time. He describes too much; but when one can describe so
well, the temptation must be great.'

That praise seems a little faint, but it is also illuminating,
because 'Tell me not here' does strike one as a poem which in
some sense has set out to 'describe' nature, as if indicating
how this should be done in terms of point and economy. More
significantly, however, the personality of the poem, which
might be taken to be assumed for a purpose, makes a sharp
contrast with the one which gives its feeling and emotion to
'Fare Well'. What is moving about de la Mare's poem is the

impression it gives of strong feelings, tendernesses, regrets, not absolutely under control, but breaking out of the lyric beauty in a manner which since Shelley ('O world! O life! O time!') could be seen as traditionally romantic. The repeated query in the first stanza, the syllabic stumble—'hand, foot, lip'—and the slight awkwardness of syntax—the 'as' in the penultimate line of the stanza Housman quoted means not 'like' but 'while', and produces a small temporary confusion of the sense—all these contribute to make us feel a poetry speaking rapidly, even breathlessly, out of the emotion of what it is saying. What is moving is not so much the thing it is saying but our sense, as readers, of this poet really feeling it. To put it thus is the natural expression of deep, recurrent impulse in his being and nature.

As the memory of things seen fades it cheers him—cheers, him fervently—to think of them being seen and enjoyed by others, especially children. This is an extremely difficult sentiment to get across, without seeming mawkish or merely well intentioned; and probably no poet other than de la Mare could do it, and do it in just this way. The poem makes a trite sentiment seem rare—rare and passionate. But one may suspect that the '*ugh!*' which was Housman's reply to those he imagined objecting to his emendation of 'rustling', carries an echo of his response to the whole poem. The thought of happy children in his haunts, and the loved and loving faces of those* who come after him, would give him no pleasure at all, any more than it would to such a poet as Larkin. But the idea might have prompted a poem of his own, in which the memory of all things lovely evokes not so much jealousy as the wry worldliness of the disillusioned lover—'I wonder who's kissing her now?' Larkin, indeed, wrote more than one poem

---

* F. W. Bateson, (*A. E. Housman: A Collection of Critical Essays*), observes that Housman could not have looked 'Fare Well' up in de la Mare's *Collected Poems*, 1920, or in an anthology, because 'if he had done so he would have found that his newspaper had committed a second misprint. De la Mare did not write 'May *these* loved and loving faces . . .' but, in opposition to 'this my dust' of the stanza's first line, 'May *those* loved and loving faces . . .'. This is interesting, because not only did Housman miss a second opportunity for emendation, but de la Mare himself may have had second thoughts, revealed in subsequent printings of the poem. The first edition of the Faber and Faber *Collected Poems* of 1942 prints 'these' and so do all subsequent impressions (ten till 1954). Either the poet changed 'those' to 'these', or he failed to notice that the printer had mistakenly done so.

on that topic, but while it produced real and anguished responses from him, from Housman in this context it can mean no more than a shrug and a smile. He can turn what might be a trite sentiment into a passion of feeling—no poet better—but he is not doing it in 'Tell me not here'. 'If truth in hearts that perish | Could move the gods on high'—that is another matter, and has something equivalent to the force and feeling of that poem de la Mare produces in his own individual way in 'Fare Well'. 'Fare Well', an essentially feeling poem, may well have produced from Housman a deliberately and meticulously stylized one, which prefers instead to enchant us with the precision of its magic.

CHAPTER 12

Contacts and Reversals

By way of epilogue let us try to make another definition, and a
further comparison. The names of Celan and Larkin have
often come up in this discussion of Housman's poems. What
these three poets incongruously have in common is the power
to break into an experience and reveal it absolutely, while at
the same time transforming it into converse truth, realized as
a poem. In their different ways all three achieve a poetry of
opposites, and of reversals. Sadness becomes cheerfulness;
horror becomes beauty; deprivation becomes fulfilment.

Poetry has always had the power to achieve such a reversal.
Shakespeare does it through style—'Those are pearls that
were his eyes'—Wordsworth through the slow build-up of a
supra-natural world, in which syntax and expression make of
the natural world their own uniquely harmonious vision. The
self-awareness of romanticism draws a particular attention to
the process, and to the way in which antitheses can be realized
in a poem, as in the Baudelairean cult of flowers out of evil.
Modernism aimed instead for what is fragmentary and
depersonalized, rejecting, as Ortega y Gasset put it, 'the
human all too human elements predominant in romantic and
naturalistic production'. Our poets' humanity, in this sense,
comes from a secret reversal, the transformation in which
their art takes place. It is part of Housman's and of Larkin's
trick to appear in a different light, which seems to intensify
their human being while releasing them from the romantic
artists' fatal seriousness about themselves.

Housman's own demure suggestion that poetry is 'best
detected' when it has no 'meaning' is a way of saying in code
that his own poetry leaves an impression contrary to its
forceful declaration of its meaning. It thrills, for instance, by
telling us there is nothing whatever in life to be thrilled about.
The 19-year-old Larkin wrote to a friend that 'life and
literature is a question of what one thrills to'. He could be

sardonic about what he thrilled to, knowing as he did what the experience was like. In a later and more aggressive mood about the affectations of late modernist poetry he said that it did not thrill him; and he and Kingsley Amis used to play at a parody of 'Fare Well' as a stock romantic poem ('Look thy last, said some old shag'). 'Seeing things as they are'* was what he felt he thrilled to; although the real thrill came from the transformation brought about by the poem as the way of seeing.

And it is through this transformation that Housman and Larkin come to life as themselves. They make no assertion of self in their poems as Emily Dickinson does, or Sylvia Plath. Plath's biographer, Anne Stevenson, was concerned to distinguish between the poet's personality in her life, and in her art. Such a distinction would mean nothing in the case of Housman or Larkin. The latter's comment on Emily Dickinson—'her inspiration derived from keeping it hidden'— is the most penetrating judgement ever made about her poetry, and it is paradoxically true about his own, if we exchange the word 'hidden' for 'transformed'. The idea of the opposite can only be unique, it is quite different from a poetic style of being. Emily Dickinson or John Berryman, Sylvia Plath or Stevie Smith, can be followed by successor poets who have learnt how to speak their idiom. No poet has learnt how to speak Housman's or Larkin's, because no one could learn how to substitute, in the secret and exclusive wiring of a poem, their positive for their negative contact. Larkin remarked that in any kind of officially sponsored poetry, 'the element of compulsive contact vanishes'. Contact in modern poets so easily becomes public and shared, a general inspiration; and this is partly because of the intellectual element in the poetry, which breeds a freemasonry of highbrow ideas, an interchange of experience and subject-matter. Housman and Larkin are not only rigorously non-intellectual in their poetic personalities, but depend upon the contemptuous exclusion of what Housman called 'lofty' matters, the kind of meditation that looks for our civilized reciprocity in *Four Quartets* or Auden's 'New Year Letter'. Their species of intelligence, and its way of getting to us, depends on excluding what Larkin called the

* *Required Writing*, 197.

'official support' of communal intelligence. Personality with them is in the operation of the seemingly furtive, of verse notionally aimed at being hidden quickly in a reader's drawer. This too, of course, is a little mocking or sardonic, as when Larkin claimed, 'we got much better poetry when it was all regarded as sinful and subversive, and you had to hide it under the cushion when somebody came in'.

Both practise an oblique but elaborate concentration on the reader getting to know them, an art of appearance which is deliberately casual and excludes any suggestion of the dramatic; although a sharply focused glimpse can reveal the poet not in relation to the reader, but with the reader as a sort of companion voyeur. The man who 'On Wenlock Edge' says 'Then, 'twas before my time, the Roman | At yonder heaving hill would stare', becomes a double voyeur with his reader. In 'Sad Steps' Larkin sees the moon, and the 'laughable' way it 'dashes through clouds that blow | Loosely as cannon-smoke to stand apart | (Stone-coloured light sharpening the roofs below)' in the same spirit. It is an art the opposite of that of the dramatic actor, suggesting a sudden blurting out which the poet deprecates, sometimes would take back if he could. At the same time there is a kind of sly, friendly satisfaction in the revelation which both parties—poet and reader—ignore, are uncertain about, or affect to be uncertain about. By such means we get to know, and the poet gets to know we know. The outburst comes to be identical with the casual suggestion ('Talking in bed ought to be easiest' or 'Strange to know nothing, never to be sure . . .'), and both suggest the primacy of a wordless state, a block that is broken by bitterness, horror, silent misery suddenly transforming themselves into excitement and delight.

> Could man be drunk for ever
>   With liquor, love, or fights,
> Lief should I rise at morning
>   And lief lie down of nights.
>
> But men at whiles are sober
>   And think by fits and starts,
> And if they think, they fasten
>   Their hands upon their hearts.
>   (*LP*, x)

The outburst appears spontaneous, a response to exasperated feeling, until the opposite effect is created in the third and fourth lines: 'lief' is a word which can only seem to be used in sudden emotion, and the faint archaism that goes with it ('of nights') suggests an equally abrupt deprecation of that response. The second verse sinks into a resignation which is also mock-comic despair at the stupidity of the human race, suffering from a sudden pain they are unable to diagnose. Or else they are showing off, claiming an emotion in romantic style. Both Larkin and Housman favour the expressive shrug, the verse that seems to make a simple, forceful point but in fact turns it into a complex one, the microcosmic display of a whole temperament. 'To put one brick upon another', a poem Larkin finally rejected for his first major collection *The Less Deceived*, sounds very like Housman:

> To put one brick upon another,
> Add a third, and then a fourth,
> Leaves no time to wonder whether
> What you do has any worth.
>
> But to sit with bricks around you
> While the winds of heaven bawl
> Weighing what you should or can do
> Leaves no doubt of it at all.

But much more like Housman is the haunting little poem of the same period called 'Days':

> What are days for?
> Days are where we live.
> They come, they wake us
> Time and time over.
> They are to be happy in:
> Where can we live but days?
>
> Ah, solving that question
> Brings the priest and the doctor
> In their long coats
> Running over the fields.

The element of deadpan oddity—the long coats, the 'lief's, the hands fastened on hearts—is essential to poems of this sort, and to 'compulsive contact' with the temperament behind it.

(Larkin underlined that temperament by writing a little parody with the query line 'What can we drink but booze?') No temperament is overtly visible in 'To put one brick upon another', only an old idea which poets like others have often had; but it shows how complex in reality are the apparently very simple poems of both poets, and how much they depend on the private glimpse of personality they afford.

It eases a horror of life in the poem's fantasy, minuscule as that fantasy may be; and balance depends on the economy, and in a sense the neatness, with which the glimpse is afforded. Celan's poems deliberately drive himself and his reader into a narrow place where the horror—and thus, in the poetry, its comfort—can be seen most intently, felt most intensely. Housman and Larkin work on the opposite principle, breaking open into pleasure, and a kind of easing, at the moment when protest is most vehement and recognition most pungent. Or the process can occur the other way round. Larkin's poem 'Wedding Wind' is a fascinated attempt by the then-youthful poet to imagine a wedding night from the bride's point of view, putting the 'poetry' in as the blowing of a great wind. 'The wind blew all, my wedding-day, | And my wedding-night was the night of the high wind . . .' Larkin's highly imaginary bride mimes the poet's own pleasure in those graceful words for the night and the day, as if by imagining them enacted (as in the marriages 'getting under way' in a later poem, 'The Whitsun Weddings') he could also participate. The undeceived poet gives himself and the reader over to a vehicle of romance, the bride asking 'Can even death dry up | These new delighted lakes? . . .', like Othello expressing his wedding joy: 'May the winds blow till they have woken death.' The poem's pleasure comes from its reversal of what the poet really thinks, a reversal made so poetically effective that it carries the poet along with it. 'Shall I be let to sleep', joyfully queries the bride, 'Now this perpetual morning shares my bed?' The poet's sense of horror at this becomes comically, but also lyrically, at one with his bride's sense of joy. The effectiveness (and originality) of the dramatic monologue is the poet's participation in his speaker's experience, and his own implicit rejection of it, not as poet but as man.

This serio-comic 'vibration', having things both ways, is not

in the normal sense ironic. But it could be a bit baffling, as it is
in Housman's 'The Land of Biscay' (*MP*, xlvi). Taking advice
from a friend who evidently was rather baffled by the tone of
this poem, Housman dropped it from *Last Poems*, and it
appeared in the posthumous collection. If the friend really
existed, and did give 'advice', he may have been bothered by a
scenario which is briefer and neater in many other poems, like
'I to my perils | Of cheat and charmer' (*MP*, vi). Such poems
embody a sly, highly crafted incongruity between manner and
matter. But like 'Wedding Wind', 'The Land of Biscay' has an
exuberant 'story' suited to the 'Laura Matilda' measure, and
with which the poet's other feelings disingenuously collude.
Starting out in his best, and most deadpan, comic vein,
Housman borrows the idea of the 'Come you all', the ballad
which calls its hearers to attend its story:

> Hearken landsmen, hearken seamen,
>   to the tale of grief and me,
> Looking from the land of Biscay
>   on the waters of the sea.

Grief, of course, is an old friend and fellow-traveller, a man to
have adventures with, the Holmes to our Watson.

> Looking from the land of Biscay
>   over Ocean to the sky
> On the far-beholding foreland
>   paced at even grief and I.

The ballad gusto is modified by dividing the long line to
subdue its trochaic metre; but the pace is as rousing as in
Tennyson's ballads, like 'The Captain' and 'The Lord of
Burghley'; even the alternations between familiar nominative
and accusative ('Grief and I' and 'Grief and me') help to keep
the show going on its apparently flamboyant journey.

> There, as warm the west was burning
>   and the east uncoloured cold,
> Down the waterway of sunset
>   drove to shore a ship of gold.

The adventure colloquy that ensues is incongruous in one
demure respect: there is no doubt of the companion's status.

Oh, said I, my friend and lover,
　　take we now that ship and sail
Outward in the ebb of hues and
　　steer upon the sunset trail;
Leave the night to fall behind us
　　and the clouding countries* leave:
Help for you and me is yonder,
　　in a haven west of eve.

The ship comes bravely on—Housman was never more skilful
in the use of his verse model.

Man and ship and sky and water
　　burning in a single flame;
And the mariner of Ocean,
　　he was calling as he came:
From the highway of the sunset
　　he was shouting on the sea,
'Landsman of the land of Biscay,
　　have you help for grief and me?'

When I heard I did not answer,
　　I stood mute and shook my head:
Son of earth and son of Ocean,
　　much we thought and nothing said.
Grief and I abode the nightfall,
　　to the sunset grief and he
Turned them from the land of Biscay
　　on the waters of the sea.

Perhaps it is hardly surprising that the friend from whom
Housman 'took advice' and dropped the poem, felt as he did.
He must have been dismayed by the incongruity between the
meaning and the motion of the poem, and the unexpected
humour that flickers through it. It is Housman's most
successful comic poem, but he himself was hardly prepared to
stand up for it, and one sees why: because part of the joke is
the deliberate laboriousness of the poetic notion, and its
development. Romantic and picturesque poetic properties are
invisibly transformed into a serio-comic opposite. 'The tale of
grief and me', the idea of grief and I as lovers, and the slow
dance of the conclusion, with one lugubrious pair standing on

* *More Poems* and *Collected Poems* have 'counties'. Archie Burnett reads 'Countries'.

the shore while the other puts to sea again, is reminiscent of
the Victorian comic classics, the Jumblies, the Dong, and the
Snark. Yet they were consciously clownish, and bidding for
pathos; and the equivocation in 'The Land of Biscay' between
the poetic and the picturesque, and the glum and comic, is
wholly individual, unique to Housman. The pathos concealed
by the poem's slightly disconcerting show of virtuosity is the
old familar one. 'Son of earth and son of Ocean | much we
thought and nothing said'. The golden sailor could be the
Friend, and our intimacy could be happily silent, happily
mutual, for both are in identical trouble. But the real friend is
not in this trouble, and any intimacy is wholly one-sided; the
poem combines the wish-fulfilment of a meeting, in an
unhappiness which is at least mutual, with a sharper
meaning, a meaning unexpectedly contrasted with the easy,
glowing picturesque. 'Every ocean smells alike of tar', in
Robert Graves's curt phrase, with which Housman would
have been in full agreement.

The notebooks show several variations and cancelled lines
in the poem, indicating a process of simplification in the
interest of the central jest. The drafts display a ship of gold,
silver, even amber, with her name on the prow and other
distractions. This accumulation is pared away in the final
poem, its economy contrasting the more effectively with the
opulence of the scene described, the brevity of the encounter
with its elaborate set-up. 'The land of Biscay' must have been
a phrase Housman was fond of, and used as a sort of talisman
in his mind for a country further off than Shropshire, which
could be endowed in imagination with the same magic power
to comfort and relieve. It is important to counter-romance
that things go as badly, or worse, in Shropshire than in other
places—'Lads knew trouble in Knighton | When I was a
Knighton lad'—and the same is true of exotic Biscay, the
point being even deftly implied in the word 'land', as opposed
to the usual 'bay'. Accurately, Biscay, with its 'far-beholding
foreland' is the furthest westerly point looking towards the
new world; and its landsmen, like their fellow-dreamers who
look towards the blue hills of Shropshire, are by a special twist
of meaning vouchsafed the sight of the golden ship from 'a
haven west of eve'.

Again there is a parallel in Larkin, a deliberately droll image of the ship drawing near which will 'heave to and unload | All good into our lives', and which is itself an engagingly grotesque apparition . . . 'leaning with brasswork prinked, | Each rope distinct, | Flagged and the figurehead with golden tits' . . . But the golden ship of 'Next, Please' never comes to our harbour.

> Only the ship is seeking us, a black-
> Sailed unfamiliar, towing at her back
> A huge and birdless silence. In her wake
> No waters breed or break.

The point, with both poets, is to extract the maximum gaiety, the most genial aesthetic 'thrill', from an end-stopped situation. It is an old tradition, but one not usually associated with the imprint of the personal which Housman and Larkin put on it. The idea of an ending may be expressed quite literally. 'Don't have any kids yourself':

> My father and my mother
> They had a likely son,
> And I have none.

The unnerving thing here is the direct application of the old idea that rosebuds fade, love is not hereafter. But the poetry can turn that cliché into something much more satisfactory: one to which every bosom returns an echo, and which goes a long way towards explaining Housman's and Larkin's popularity. Grief, like work, is its own reward, its own way of saying there is nothing to be said. 'Give me your arm, old toad' . . . The amusing thing about 'the scorned unlucky lad' is that he 'Mans his hearts and deep and glad | Drinks the valiant air of morn'. The new start is the same as the old ending.

The poet's instinct for finality is also the need for enclosure. Larkin starts many exploratory poems, like the slow-motion one called 'The Dance'. Its funereal but fascinating accumulation of detail and impression has no place to go, and breaks off while the dance, with its apparently genuine invitation to life and love, is still going on. The poet is aware of 'a whole consenting language', 'a tremendous answer banging back'; but his attempt to define it all to himself leads him into the

language-world of a novel, away from the self-definition
needed by his kind of poem. The idea of possibility remains
equally seductive to Housman, and equally unavailable to his
poetry, except as the possibility of 'a tremendous answer'
suggested by the very limitations of the poem. Housman's
athlete, that 'smart lad', was right 'to slip betimes away',
because winning does not allow for further 'development':

> Eyes the shady night has shut
> Cannot see the record cut . . .

The word 'cut' has a particular force which might stand for all
such operations in Housman's poetry, appropriate equally to
film language today and to the slang of competitive athletics
in Housman's time. The poem exists in its own enclave in
order that, like the athlete, it should not have to see other
possibilities.

But his poems reflect the fact that Housman himself had
two kinds of possibility to contemplate. One was that of Moses
Jackson: what would have happened if, instead of 'grief and I'
setting off for a chat with 'grief and me', he, the poet, had been
loved? The other, which had a paradoxical similarity, was the
challenge offered by the classics; and the certainty, never to be
proved, that he had found out the actual words written by a
Roman poet, words written not for him 'because the Romans
are foreigners and write to please themselves, not us'. His love
for Jackson and his love for the text of Manilius had
something in common. Jackson lived to please himself, not
Housman. Absorption in the young man met as a student, and
in the words of the Roman poet, had in common the complete
indifference of its object, an indifference which in itself
absolutely validated the genuineness of the absorption, and
set it apart from any other pursuit or feeling.

'A scientist and athlete whose contempt for letters was
unconcealed.' So A. S. F. Gow, Housman's friend and fellow
classical scholar, described Moses Jackson. In Larkin's poem
'Wild Oats' | 'a bosomy English rose' came in 'about twenty
years ago' to the place where he worked, and is commemorated
by two snapshots in his wallet. 'Unlucky charms, perhaps.'
We can be sure that the English rose had not the smallest
interest in poetry, as she had none in the poet. In both cases

the unlucky love lasted, and so do the poems it produced. Only unlucky love could have sealed off the area in which the poetry was secreted like the pearl inside the shell.

The sealed enclosure, in which both poets alone can operate successfully, keeps out the poetical. In terms of our contemporary poetical speech it is a striking thing that the more open a poem, the more hospitable—perhaps conscientiously so—to everyday life and the concerns of communal living, the more it comes to depend on its own form of poetical or 'Parnassian' speech. By welcoming everyday life it causes everyday life to give a welcome back, and the result is a conspiracy of the poetical, found, for example, in the poetry of John Ashbery, a poet who might seem at first to have something in common both with Larkin and with Housman. But their secret is in complete indifference, the indifference of the desired object to themselves finding its correlative in the seeming indifference of poem to reader. And this disregard is expressed in the ways it conveys a refusal to enter into predictable poetic relationship. John Berryman, Elizabeth Bishop, John Ashbery—many more—all set up that relationship, and with an elaborateness which is part of the reward of their poetry, and its pleasure. They are open to the reader, as they seem open to the whole of life.

Housman and Larkin are not. They represent, and with singular emphasis, the enclosed, as opposed to the open, category of poetry: and communication with them depends on surprise. It depends on a relation strikingly similar to what might happen if Housman's indifferent scientist and athlete, or Larkin's 'English rose' trying not to laugh, were suddenly to take an interest in what the poet is feeling and saying—were to hang, in fact, upon his lips. Such a seemingly impossible reciprocity must have thrilled Housman when he discovered that young men who had never cared about poetry found themselves hooked on *A Shropshire Lad*. The secret hope of Larkin's poetry, too, is that the reader might begin by being as uninterested as that 'English rose', and then be suddenly startled to find that he or she isn't.

For both poets enclosure is also an absence. Their sealed-off world is none the less never claustrophobic, and never feels it. The paradox in Celan, too, is that the narrow place, the

'Engführung', also seems, with the words that measure it, wide with nothingness. When Larkin writes of 'Such attics cleared of me! Such absences!'—the absence looks beyond the words, and beyond the business of poetry, of being a poet. It can also look beyond the experience or feeling that struck the poet and that he wishes to give us, as in 'High Windows'. What strikes him there is that the young always seem free and emancipated to the old; but with that fairly familiar idea, 'Rather than words comes the thought of high windows: | The sun-comprehending glass'. Nothing might seem more 'poetical' than that epithet; but like Housman's 'twelve-winded', it appears to vanish into the achieved absence of the poem. The two poets clear off back to the office and the library, the daily job.

Even mannerism in them can breed absence. Like Larkin's use of coarse colloquialisms ('seeing things as they are'), Housman's vocabulary, with its smart lads and clean endings, does not seem a way of evading the poetical, and neither does it lay a self-conscious emphasis on his own version of it. True, in both cases it serves to remind us that the normal fiddle of poetry is not going on here, but neither is any crude substitute for it. The suicide's grave in Housman is not a place of gloating literary association, nor an image of personal misery, but a light, enchanting spot, a perpetual absence in sunlight where the nettle performs its dance devoid of meaning.

As his lines expose themselves, and as we expose ourselves to them and to what is in them, we do not feel, any more than we do with Larkin, that Housman's is a limited and arrested kind of poetry. The emotion in it is too strong to resolve itself, but this stoic inability is a source of endless fascination and humour, and of a poetry becoming rich on rejection. In a lecture on 'The application of Thought to Textual Criticism', given to the Classical Association in Cambridge in 1921, Housman tells us how to detect a *non sequitur*, the example given being that of some classical scholar who has laid it down that 'Interpolation is, speaking generally, comparatively an uncommon source of alteration, and we should therefore be loth to assume it in a given case'. Should we? observes Housman. Suppose we read that 'a bullet-wound is, speaking generally, comparatively an uncommon cause of death, and we should therefore be loth to assume it in a given case'. What if the given case were death on a battlefield? Should we suppose it to be caused by tuberculosis, the commonest cause of death among the young? What would be thought of someone who concluded that? 'Well, it would probably be thought that he was a textual critic strayed from home.'

The example is revealing, for Housman in his poetry is a textual critic who has strayed from home on to the battlefield. But, more than that, he is tacitly kind both to his own obsession and to the critic of the *non sequitur* who has strayed from home and become part of the general misfitness of things. His severity, like that of Larkin, whose 'Homage to a Government' is the equivalent of Housman's poem on the Queen's Jubilee, '1887', is tempered by a shrug. Yet his fellow-feeling surfaces in unexpected places, outside the necessary enclosure of his poems but related to them by an undercover route. The friendly letter to his fellow scholar Gilbert Murray (April 1900), doubts if 'man really has much to gain by substituting peace for strife, as you and Jesus Christ recommend'. Housman never talks like that in a poem, and he is never in fact blasphemous in them, for blasphemy involves a deliberate trailing of the coat, which can be done to a fellow classics professor but not to an audience of young men. Shy of vehemence, whether in friends or in poets, they would respond to Housman's skill in putting strong feelings and shocking beliefs obliquely and by contrasts. Walter de la Mare could express what he felt with a directness and fervour quite alien to Housman, who in 'Tell me not here' conveys his love of beauty in a deliberate turning away from her charms. All these devices and desires of the poet were censured in various ways by a younger generation of critics, who were repelled by affectation and sincerity alike, and by the disconcerting way they mingled. The achievement of a poem like 'The Land of Biscay' would have been totally misunderstood, even by the new critics. But now the heat of controversy has died down; with both attackers and defenders departed Housman can be enjoyed with the detachment of true interest, as personality and as poet.

What is his place today? His popularity, like Larkin's, results from his own use of a convention as old as the art itself:

the lament, the complaint, the sad ballad. Poetry brings comfort by the way it celebrates despair and the sadness of things. That is obvious, but Housman was very particular about it being done in the right way. The point of 'Sorrow, that is not sorrow, but delight', the line from Wordsworth which Housman significantly quoted in 'The Name and Nature of Poetry', is that only poetry can produce it. From the popularity of *The Shropshire Lad* Housman knew that he had succeeded in producing it himself. His own estimate of his powers is never referred to, never on the surface, but the implication is there. Heroism is the response to the sadness of things, and poetry can embody it, whether in Job, or the Iliad, in Celan, or in a lyric of Shelley. Housman invented a new heroic theme, the Shropshire theme, and his admirer John Berryman was right to identify that new version of heroes. Larkin also invented a new heroic theme, the joys of routine and deprivation. The man who takes the arm of the toad, work, is like Achilles putting on his armour, or like Housman's heroes—'The sure, the straight, the brave'— bracing their belts about them. Again the implication is there, and it is part of a joke, a joke which reveals the attitude and the art needful to heroic stylization. 'Stand, quit you like stone, be strong.'

> Out of the day and night
> A joy has taken flight:

The joy that was promised was advertised by Larkin's girl on the poster *Come to Sunny Prestatyn*, the girl 'too good for this life'. Poetry, as Housman and as Larkin understand it, is 'too good for this life', which is why it is best suited to the heroic ideal. In both poets that ideal is presented with undercover hilarity, imaged in Shropshire, in the names taken from guidebooks, in the finality of death, the failures with men or with girls. The heroic ideal in modern poetry makes up its own sort of shorthand, which can be 'read' before it is understood.

> The chestnut casts his flambeaux, and the flowers
> Stream from the hawthorn on the wind away,
> The doors clap to, the pane is blind with showers.
> Pass me the can, lad; there's an end of May.
>
> (*LP*, ix)

The setting is instant: but heroism is underscored by being sent up. 'Whatever brute or blackguard made the world', like Larkin's 'shit in the shuttered chateau', is a creation both potent and grotesque. He has hurled our hopeful plans to emptiness and made us sit in the pub in the downpour while he might be out playing cricket. These are the troubles of our proud and angry dust, and of the fact that 'no pair of kings our mothers bore'. Reversed heroism is the same shorthand as truth by denial, which we get two poems later on:

> Oh often have I washed and dressed
>   And what's to show for all my pain?
> Let me lie abed and rest:
> Ten thousand times I've done my best
>   And all's to do again.
>
> *(LP, xi)*

There is a great deal to show, as he well knows; but to stretch out for a moment, as he does in the shortened stress of the third line, is the impulse that matters. Let Larkin have the last word.

> She kept her songs, they took so little space,
>   The covers pleased her:
> One bleached from lying in a sunny place,
> One marked in circles by a vase of water,
> One mended when a tidy fit had seized her,
>   And coloured, by her daughter—
> So they had waited, till in widowhood
> She found them, looking for something else, and stood
> Relearning how each frank submissive chord
>   Had ushered in
> Word after sprawling hyphenated word . . .

'Love Songs in Age' revisits 'the unfailing sense of being young', and the scene of 'that much-mentioned brilliance, love',

> Still promising to solve, and satisfy,
> And set unchangeably in order. So
>   To pile them back, to cry,
> Was hard, without lamely admitting how
> It had not done so then, and could not now.

As Housman might have recognized, whether he liked the poem or not, the heroic mode here is feeling its way with great nerve into a situation in which it is not supposed to feel at all at home. A marriage, a family, widowhood, the give and take of domestic life, are played against heroic absolutes—youth, hope, art and song, grief and failure. Love too. Did love do nothing? The poem shows that it did, by stating, to its own and to our satisfaction, that it had not done, and could not do so. Housman's poems, in the end, can be seen to perform much the same feat.

Bibliography

ABRAMS, M. H., *The Mirror and the Lamp* (New York, 1953).

AIKEN, CONRAD, 'A. E. Housman', *New Republic* (Nov. 1936).

ALLISON, A. F., 'The Poetry of A. E. Housman', *Review of English Studies*, 19 (1943).

BARFIELD, OWEN, *Poetic Diction* (London, 1934).

BLACKMAN, R. P., *The Expense of Greatness* (Gloucester, Mass., 1958).

BRINDLE, C. O., *English Classical Scholarship: Reflections on Bentley, Polson Housman* (London, 1986).

BROOKS, CLEANTH, 'The Whole of Housman', *Kenyon Review*, 3 (1941).

CARTER, JOHN, 'The Text of Housman's Poems', *Times Literary Supplement* (15 June, 1956).

—— *A. E. Housman: Selected Prose* (London, 1961).

—— and JOHN SPARROW (eds.), *A. E. Housman: A Bibliography*, 2nd edn. revised by William White (London, 1982).

CHAMBERS, R. W., 'A. E. Housman', in *Man's Unconquerable Mind* (London, 1939).

COCKERELL, SYDNEY, 'Dates of Housman Poems', *Times Literary Supplement* (7 Nov. 1936); repr. in Grant Richard's *Housman: 1897–1936* (London, 1941).

CONNOLLY, CYRIL, 'A. E. Housman: A Controversy', in *The Condemned Playground* (London, 1946); repr. in Ricks (ed.), *A. E. Housman: A Collection of Critical Essays* (London, 1968).

DIGGLE J. and GOODYEAR, F. R. D., *The Classical Papers of A. E. Housman*, 3 vols. (Cambridge, 1972).

DOBRÉE, BONAMY, 'The Complete Housman', *Spectator*, 164 (5 Jan. 1940).

EDWARDS, MICHAEL, *Poetry and Possibility* (London, 1988).

EMPSON, WILLIAM, *Some Versions of Pastoral* (London, 1935).

GARROD, H. W., 'Mr A. E. Housman', *The Profession of Poetry and Other Lectures* (Oxford, 1929).

GOW, A. S. F., *A. E. Housman: A Sketch* (London, 1936).

GRAVES, RICHARD PERCEVAL, *A. E. Housman: The Scholar Poet* (London, 1979).

HABER, TOM BURNS, *The Manuscript Poems of A. E. Housman* (Minneapolis, 1955).

—— *The Making of A Shropshire Lad* (Seattle, 1966).

—— *A. E. Housman* (New York, 1967).

HOUSMAN, LAURENCE, *A. E. H.* (London, 1937).

HOUSMAN, LAURENCE, 'A. E. Housman's "De Amicitia" ', *Encounter* (Oct. 1967).

JARRELL, RANDALL, 'Texts from Housman' *Kenyon Review*, 1 (1939), repr. in *Encounter* (Oct. 1967) and Ricks (ed.), *A. E. Housman: A Collection of Critical Essays* (London, 1968).

LARKIN, PHILIP, *Required Writing: Miscellaneous Pieces 1955–1982* (London, 1982).

LEGGETT, B. J., *Housman's Land of Lost Content* (London, 1970).

—— *The Poetic Art of A. E. Housman* (London, 1978).

LUCAS, F. L., *The Decline and Fall of the Romantic Ideal* (London, 1936).

—— 'A. E. Housman's Poetry', *New Statesman and Nation* (30 May, 1936).

MAAS, HENRY, *The Letters of A. E. Housman* (London, 1971).

MARLOW, NORMAN, *A. E. Housman, Scholar and Poet* (London, 1958).

MONRO, HAROLD, *Some Contemporary Poets* (London, 1920).

NAIDITCH, P., 'Housman's Letters', *Housman Society Journal*, 9 (1983).

PAGE, NORMAN, *A. E. Housman: A Critical Biography* (London, 1983).

POUND, EZRA, 'Mr Housman at Little Bethel', *Criterion*, 13 (1934).

RANSOM, JOHN CROWE, 'Honey and Gall', *Southern Review*, 6 (1940).

RICHARDS, GRANT, *Housman: 1897–1936* (London, 1941).

RICKS, CHRISTOPHER (ed.), *A. E. Housman: A Collection of Critical Essays* (London, 1968)—includes his 'The Nature of Housman's Poetry', repr. from *Essays in Criticism*, 14 (1964).

—— *The Force of Poetry* (Oxford, 1984).

—— (ed.), *A. E. Housman: Collected Poems and Selected Prose*, with an Introduction and Notes (Harmondsworth, 1988).

SPARROW, JOHN, Introduction to *Collected Poems of A. E. Housman* (London, 1956).

Index